PUTTING OUT FIRES

A Framework for Solving Problems in Your Classroom or School

KAYLAH HOLLAND

INTERNATIONAL SOCIETY FOR TECHNOLOGY IN EDUCATION
ARLINGTON, VIRGINIA

Putting Out Fires
A Framework for Solving Problems in Your Classroom or School
Kaylah Holland

Director of Books and Journals: *Emily Reed*
Senior Acquisitions Editor: *Valerie Witte*
Copy Editor: *Courtney Burkholder*
Proofreader: *Emily Padgett*
Indexer: *Kento Ikeda*
Book Design and Production: *Danielle Foster*
Cover Design: *Tonika Carter, Beth Schlenoff*

Library of Congress Cataloging-in-Publication Data
Names: Holland, Kaylah, author.
Title: Putting out fires : a framework for solving problems in your classroom or school / Kaylah Holland.
Description: First edition. | Arlington, Virginia : International Society for Technology in Education, 2024. | Includes bibliographical references and index.
Identifiers: LCCN 2024016048 (print) | LCCN 2024016049 (ebook) | ISBN 9798888370285 (paperback) | ISBN 9798888370261 (epub) | ISBN 9798888370278 (pdf)
Subjects: LCSH: Classroom management. | School management and organization. | Classroom environment. | School environment. | Problem solving.
Classification: LCC LB3013 .H64125 2024 (print) | LCC LB3013 (ebook) | DDC 371.102/4—dc23/eng/20240507
LC record available at https://lccn.loc.gov/2024016048
LC ebook record available at https://lccn.loc.gov/2024016049

First Edition

ISBN: 9798888370285

Ebook version available

Printed in the United States of America

ISTE® is a registered trademark of the International Society for Technology in Education.

ABOUT ISTE

The International Society for Technology in Education (ISTE) is home to a passionate community of global educators who believe in the power of technology to transform teaching and learning, accelerate innovation, and solve tough problems in education.

ISTE inspires the creation of solutions and connections that improve opportunities for all learners by delivering practical guidance, evidence-based professional learning, virtual networks, thought-provoking events, and the ISTE Standards. ISTE is also the leading publisher of books focused on technology in education. For more information or to become an ISTE member, visit iste.org. Subscribe to ISTE's YouTube channel, and connect with ISTE on X, Facebook, and LinkedIn.

RELATED ISTE TITLES

Elevate Equity in Edtech: Expanding Inclusive Leadership Through the ISTE Standards by Victoria Thompson (ISTE, 2024)

Inclusive Learning 365: Edtech Strategies for Every Day of the Year by Christopher Bugaj, Karen Janowski, Mike Marotta, and Beth Poss (ISTE, 2021)

To see all books available from ISTE, please visit iste.org/books.

PUBLISHER'S ACKNOWLEDGMENTS

ISTE gratefully acknowledges the contributions of the following reviewers:

Susan Herder
Valerie Janowski
Marina Lombardo
Kristy Nelson

ABOUT THE AUTHOR

 **Kaylah Holland, Ed.D** is passionate about empowering educators through professional development, one-on-one coaching, and innovative lesson design. She holds a doctorate in education in the field of Instructional Design and Technology with a focus on active learning environments. Driven by a passion for education, Holland consistently explores innovative methods to empower educators and champion student-centered classrooms. She is a Google Certified Innovator, Trainer, and Coach; a college professor; and an ISTE Community Leader. She was presented ISTE's "20 to Watch" award in 2022 and was recognized by *EdTech K–12 Magazine* as a top 30 influencer in 2023. As the director of Instructional Technology and Blended Learning for BreakFree Education, Holland empowers educators to foster innovative, sustainable, and active educational experiences inside juvenile justice facilities across the United States, offering students held in confinement a path to success in school and life. She also advocates for equitable access to education across the globe as the founder of Go Teach Be Love and the co-founder of Global Good EDU.

ACKNOWLEDGMENTS

Kat Crawford, I'd like to thank you for your invaluable contributions to the *Putting Out Fires* Framework. We created this framework together after countless discussions and shared insights. Your creativity and innovative ideas have enriched the framework in many ways, and I am proud to acknowledge your pivotal role in its creation.

DEDICATION

This book is dedicated to the incredibly hardworking educators serving justice-involved youth in secure schools across the United States. These educators dedicate themselves to ensuring *all* students have a path to success in both school and life. I am endlessly inspired by their passion, resilience, and tireless commitment to education.

I also dedicate this book to my mom—your love, wisdom, and steadfast belief in my potential has fueled my journey. This book is a tribute to the incredible strength and guidance you have provided me, and is a testament to your unwavering belief that anything is possible.

TABLE OF CONTENTS

PREFACE   X

CHAPTER 1
SUITING UP   1

Design Thinking. 3

The Process 4

How to Use This Book. 6

Fire Drill!. 9

Sample Problems 11

What Happens Next?. 12

CHAPTER 2
WHAT'S YOUR PROBLEM?   13

Upstream Thinking. 14

Barriers to Upstream Thinking .17

Selecting the Right Problem. 19

Fire Drill!. 23

Sample Problems 26

What Happens Next?. 32

CHAPTER 3
PEOPLE AT THE CENTER   33

Keep People at the Center 36

Fire Drill! 37

Sample Problems 39

What Happens Next? 44

CHAPTER 4
THE PUTTING OUT FIRES FRAMEWORK   45

Levels of Capacity and Influence 48

Fire Drill! 50

Sample Problems 53

What Happens Next? 60

CHAPTER 5
EXTINGUISH THE EMBERS   61

Innovative Extinguish Solutions 64

Fire Drill! 66

Sample Problems 69

What Happens Next? 74

CHAPTER 6
DETECT THE FLAMES 75

An Innovative Detect Solution. 77

Fire Drill!. 79

Sample Problems 82

What Happens Next?. 87

CHAPTER 7
CONTAIN THE BLAZE 89

An Innovative Contain Solution. 91

Fire Drill!. 93

Sample Problems 96

What Happens Next?. 101

CHAPTER 8
PREVENT THE FIRESTORM 103

An Innovative Prevent Solution 106

Fire Drill!. 108

Sample Problems 111

What Happens Next?. 116

CHAPTER 9
PUTTING OUT THE FIRE 117

Clear the Path 118

Implementation Strategies 120

Fire Drill! 123

Sample Problems 124

What Happens Next? 128

CHAPTER 10
WHEN THE SMOKE CLEARS 129

Obtaining Feedback 130

Reflecting on the Process 131

Fire Drill! 132

Sample Problems 134

CONCLUSION 138

REFERENCES 139

INDEX 141

PREFACE

IF THIS FRAMEWORK WORKS IN JUVENILE JUSTICE CLASSROOMS, IT CAN WORK ANYWHERE!

My greatest passions are creating active learning experiences and designing student-centered educational environments. I have extensive experience working in unique educational environments, including secure schools and international schools. I strive to improve education for students confined in the US juvenile justice (US JJ) system and work diligently to provide purposeful professional development to educators around the world. I, along with Kat Crawford, created the framework found within this book as a response to the consistent problems educators face working in the US JJ system.

Education inside the US JJ system is littered with obstacles teachers must overcome to make learning happen. Education inside JJ facilities is provided at a secure school. To access the secure school, teachers enter and exit a locked facility such as a jail or detention center daily. They teach students with access to very few resources, and they often teach multiple grade levels at once. Despite these challenges, there are incredible teachers working inside secure schools across the country, helping students thrive using lessons that are engaging, relevant, and meaningful. The *Putting Out Fires* Framework offered in this book has helped teachers in secure schools solve problems by implementing creative practical solutions; it will very likely work for you and your school. I do not mean to belittle your specific challenges. Educators everywhere face problems every single day—but educators in secure schools experience the problems you typically face and many more. This framework works for JJ teachers, and it can work for you, too!

CHAPTER 1
SUITING UP

THE ALARM SOUNDS. Firefighters rush to don their protective gear. When they suit up, they understand their purpose in the world changes. They are no longer average folks going about their day—driving to work, running errands, mowing the lawn, or cooking dinner. When they suit up, firefighters understand they may be fighting a dangerous fire, and their mindset shifts, enabling them to complete safety checks and ensure team members are prepared before running into a burning building, saving lives, and extinguishing the fire.

I work with teachers in secure schools across the United States. When I ask them how they are doing, I often get the same response: "Oh, you know, I'm just putting out fires." Many teachers in secure schools feel like they spend most or all of their time solving problems. Maybe you can relate to this feeling; I know I can.

Why do educators feel like they are constantly solving problems? Why do educators feel that these problems are the same problems they solved yesterday and the day before and the day before that? What makes these problems persist the way they do? The *Putting Out Fires* Framework outlined in this book will help you discover the root causes of persistent problems and create lasting solutions. Can this book solve all the world's problems? No, but what this book *can* do is present a process that encourages you to shift your mindset in order to create sustainable change in your classrooms and schools. The *Putting Out Fires* Framework encourages you to select a specific problem, discover its core causes and symptoms, uncover everyone affected by the problem, and create a practical, sustainable solution. I truly believe that you can break the cycle of constantly putting out fires. I'll show you how to implement sustainable solutions to problems so they do not crop up again and again.

Before we get started, it's time to put on your firefighting gear. You are no longer a regular teacher or administrator going about the day—grading assignments, creating lesson plans, attending meetings, and advocating for students. You are now preparing to fight a fire—by which I mean a persistent problem. The process outlined over the next several chapters may seem overwhelming at first, but it will present a path forward that is easy to understand and that excites you with its potential. Completing the process will break the current cycle of ineffective responses to recurring issues and will become your own personal firefighting gear as you begin to tackle challenges.

DESIGN THINKING

The *Putting Out Fires* Framework was created specifically to leverage the design-thinking process to assist educators in solving problems. While there is no single definition of *design thinking*, it is widely recognized as a way of thinking, a process, and a path forward that allows people using the design thinking process to view problems in a new way while keeping humans at the center. Tim Brown, chair of IDEO, says that design thinking is a "human-centered approach to innovation that draws from the designer's toolkit to integrate the needs of people, the possibilities of technology, and the requirements for business success" (n.d.). Design thinking allows people who may not consider themselves to be creative to address challenges using creative tools, "[bringing] together what is desirable from a human point of view with what is technologically feasible and economically viable" (IDEO, n.d.). IDEO is considered the current leader in design thinking, but the process has existed for decades. We know that "early glimpses of design thinking date back to the 1950s and 60s, although these references were more within the context of architecture and engineering" (Dam and Siang, 2022). We also know that World War II had a "profound effect on strategic thinking, . . . and we have looked for new ways to solve complex problems ever since" (Dam and Siang, 2022). In the 1960s, '70s, and '80s, many notable people began connecting design to problem solving, including cognitive scientist Herbert A. Simon. In 1969, Simon published a book, *The Sciences of the Artificial*, in which he was the first to connect design to a way of thinking. Simon contributed "many ideas throughout the 1970s which are now regarded as principles of design thinking" (Dam and Siang, 2022), including rapid prototyping, an activity you will complete in a future chapter. One reason design thinking was used as a basis for the framework is that the process helps you remain focused on solutions instead of problems. If we place our focus on the problem itself, we often become stuck complaining about the problem without actually creating action steps to solve it. In the 1980s, Bryan Lawson concluded that "scientists were problem-focused problem-solvers whereas the designers were solution-focused" (Dam and Siang, 2022).

In 1991, IDEO was founded. They quickly injected design thinking into areas other than business and science by creating a user-friendly path to success for those without a degree in design methodology. In 2004 "David Kelley founded the Hasso Plattner Institute of Design at Stanford—commonly known as the d.school" (Dam and Siang, 2022). IDEO and the d.school are both excellent resources for learning more about design thinking. For the purposes of this book, design thinking may be viewed as a process of looking deeply into problems while keeping people at the center of the process and remaining solution focused.

The *Putting Out Fires* Framework uses design thinking to explore the true causes of a problem and discover all potential solutions for it. With numerous activities to complete for separate steps in the process, this book offers many ways to practice design thinking. The *Putting Out Fires* Framework includes activities specifically curated or created for educators solving problems. The activities in this book delve deeply into current problems in education to learn about the causes and symptoms, keep humans at the center of the process, stay focused on solutions, and create practical action steps for implementing a successful solution.

THE PROCESS

The process outlined in this book allows you to tackle a specific, current problem in your classroom, school, or personal life. In the following chapters you will complete the process outlined in **Figure 1.1** by selecting a problem and determining the actual root cause of that problem; by acknowledging the people involved and determining your true assumptions about those people; and by creating numerous solutions and categorizing those solutions according to the *Putting Out Fires* Framework (see **Figure 1.2**). This framework looks at the potential of and your influence on each solution. The process ends by guiding you through the implementation of one specific solution and asking you to reflect on the impact of that solution to determine if it was successful.

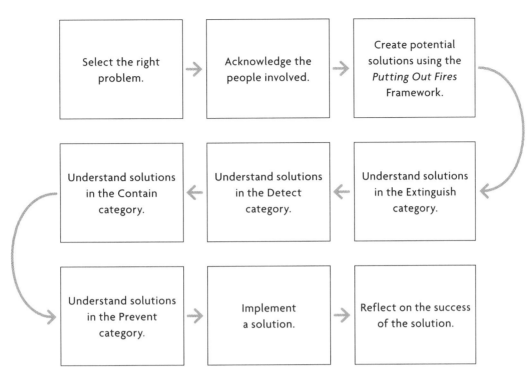

FIGURE 1.1 The *Putting Out Fires* Problem-Solving Process.

FIGURE 1.2 The *Putting Out Fires* Framework.

HOW TO USE THIS BOOK

Each forthcoming chapter highlights one of the steps from the *Putting Out Fires* Framework and includes three sections. The first section contains content to help you better understand the step highlighted in the chapter and why the step is important to the overall process. This content section also includes innovative and interesting real-world examples of problem solving at its finest.

The second section of each chapter is called Fire Drill! In this section, you will apply what you have learned in the chapter by completing practical design-thinking activities. These learning opportunities are engaging, relevant, and meaningful, and each of the activities has a genuine purpose and is crucial to the overall process. The Fire Drill! section includes instructions on how to complete each activity. In addition to written instructions, you can scan an associated QR code to hear important instructions and reminders.

The third section of each chapter contains sample problems. To ensure you understand the process and complete the activities correctly, I have included one problem a teacher might face and one problem an administrator might face regarding the use of educational technology. You will see how the Fire Drill! activities were completed for the two sample problems, allowing you to use these examples as a guide when applying the process.

To round out this chapter, we'll look at a sample Fire Drill! and sample problems.

CONNECTION TO ISTE STANDARDS

The content in this book directly aligns with the ISTE Standards, particularly the sections of the standards for educators and education leaders. Sample problems are placed at the end of each chapter to help you view problem-solving activities in action. Each of the sample problems will be connected to the appropriate ISTE standard.

Standards Connections for Educators

Using design thinking and the *Putting Out Fires* Framework to understand problems and create potential solutions allows teachers to become:

- learners exploring new ways to create a better learning environment,
- leaders seeking new opportunities to improve teaching and learning,
- citizens creating socially responsible students who positively contribute to issues in our world,
- analysts understanding root causes and collecting data behind current problems in order to implement the most effective solution, and
- designers creating authentic solutions to real problems taking place in your classrooms (ISTE, 2017).

Standards Connections for Education Leaders

Using design thinking and the *Putting Out Fires* Framework to understand problems and create potential solutions allows administrators to:

- advocate for proper equity in their schools,
- design a strategic vision engaging stakeholders and empowering all voices,
- create a culture that inspires innovation,
- build sustainability through implementing effective systems, and
- model best practices for continuous learning (ISTE, 2018).

Learn more about the ISTE standards at **iste.org/standards**.

ADDITIONAL RESOURCES

QR codes are included in the workbook sections of each chapter to add to the overall experience. Scan the QR codes to access audio instructions before completing the activities at the end of each chapter.

A companion website includes resources consulted when researching and writing the book. The companion website will continuously be updated. Access the website at www.kaylahholland.com/puttingoutfires.

CONNECT WITH ME

I am passionate about innovative problem solving and providing the absolute best experiences for students. I truly believe that we learn better together and would love to know more about your selected problems and potential solutions. If you would like to share your process as you complete the activities in this book, please do so on any social media platform. When sharing please tag @hollandkaylah and use #puttingoutfires. You can also reach out directly on social media @hollandkaylah, or through the website at **www.kaylahholland.com/puttingoutfires**.

🔔 FIRE DRILL!

Welcome to your first Fire Drill! You can now put into practice what you've learned throughout this chapter. This section in Chapter 1 serves as an example of what the Fire Drill! sections will include in each of the upcoming chapters. Your first step is to read the instructions (as you are now doing). The second step is to scan the QR code to the right to hear more detailed information from the author about the specific activities in each Fire Drill! section.

kaylahholland.com/
puttingoutfires/audio

ACTIVITIES

In the third and final step, you will complete the activities listed below. Some chapters will have one activity, while others will have several. As you progress through the book, each Fire Drill! will bring you closer to implementing a sustainable solution to a real problem you are experiencing, using the process outlined in **Figure 1.1** earlier in this chapter.

THINKING AND FEELING

Complete the following steps to better understand where your brain and heart are before beginning this process.

- Set a timer for one minute.
- Using the space provided, write down your thoughts as you embark on this journey. Thinking uses our brains and logic. Perhaps you are thinking you might not have time to complete this entire process, or you are wondering how fast you can finish this book because you need a solution right away.
- Next set a timer for one minute and in the blank space under "Feeling" draw a visual representation of how you feel about starting this journey. Feeling comes from our heart and emotions. Are you excited, hopeful, or nervous (Bolger, 2022)?

Once you have completed the Fire Drill! activities, continue to the next section to see these activities completed for two sample problems.

THINKING

_____

_____

_____

_____

_____

_____

_____

_____

FEELING

SAMPLE PROBLEMS

The Sample Problems section concludes each chapter, serving as a guide to completing the Fire Drill! activities and offering a glimpse into how actual problems move through the *Putting Out Fires* process. The same two problems will be highlighted in the Sample Problems section of each forthcoming chapter. One sample problem is specific to teachers, and the other is geared toward administrators. This section will also highlight how each sample problem is aligned to appropriate ISTE standards. Read the brief descriptions of the two sample problems below.

TEACHERS: PURPOSEFUL TECHNOLOGY USE TO ENHANCE STUDENT LEARNING

When focusing on the use of technology in education, teachers consistently face challenges. These include a lack of professional development, outdated devices (or no devices at all), complicated digital programs, equitable access, and more. The sample problem for teachers will specifically address the challenge of how to engage students in the classroom using technology, and will emphasize best practices for blending technology seamlessly into the classroom while engaging students with the purposeful use of technology to enhance their learning experience. This problem is important because we need to equip students with skills such as digital literacy, critical thinking, and problem solving. Focusing on the purposeful use of technology as the problem will allow for the design of innovative solutions that will enhance student learning.

ADMINISTRATORS: ENSURING SCHOOLWIDE TECHNOLOGY PROGRAMS MEET THE NEEDS OF DIVERSE LEARNERS

When focusing on the use of technology in education, administrators face many challenges, including a lack of professional development, budget constraints, security concerns, creating equitable policies, and more. The sample problem for administrators will specifically address the challenge of creating school-wide technology programs that meet the needs of diverse learners. This multi-faceted problem might include cultural sensitivity, adaptive learning tools, language barriers, and restructuring policies to be less punitive. This problem is important because we must ensure the technology devices and programs provided meet the needs of all learner, allowing every student to succeed.

WHAT HAPPENS NEXT?

You now understand the plan and process for the remainder of this book. The next step is to get started. The fire alarm is ringing, so suit up. Let's go.

CHAPTER 2
WHAT'S YOUR PROBLEM?

ALL PROBLEMS ARE NOT CREATED EQUAL. Some need immediate attention, while others need more careful thought and planning to implement a solution with long-term impact. Some affect one person, while others affect many. Often, when we approach problem solving, we move too quickly, forgetting to step back to understand the breadth and depth of the problem, acknowledging both the causes and symptoms. In the moment, we simply want the problem solved, but not all problems can be fully solved with an immediate solution. When we change our mindset from "I must solve this problem now" to "I must fully understand the problem and implement a solution that will have the largest positive impact," we begin to think like a designer. A designer takes time to understand every nuance of a problem before implementing a carefully-considered solution. If you are reading this book, you are ready to think like a designer when creating solutions for existing problems. When we begin with a designer's mindset, the end solution will have a greater impact.

UPSTREAM THINKING

In 2020 Dan Heath published a book called *Upstream: The Quest to Solve Problems before They Happen.* As an avid design thinker and problem solver, I was intrigued by the title, and after reading *Upstream*, my mindset around problem solving was forever changed. The main idea in *Upstream* is that problems are like a river, and the farther upstream you go, the more multiple solutions become apparent, and the more likely the solution(s) you implement will have profound and lasting effects. Heath notes that this idea had its genesis in a public health parable commonly attributed to Irving Zola. In the parable, two people are fishing along a riverbank when they see a drowning child being swept down the river. They quickly jump into the river to save the drowning child. Back on the riverbank, they see another child being swept down the river. They save the second child but see another child, then another, then another, and before they know it, they are stuck in a cycle of response, saving one child at a time. Eventually, one of the two people starts upriver, and the other asks where they are going. The departing rescuer says, "I'm going upstream to find the person throwing all the kids in the river" (Heath, 2020).

When a problem arises, we often implement the first, most obvious solution, and feel virtuous—only to have the problem quickly return. When under pressure, the obvious solution to any given problem tends to be the one we go with first. The idea that there are likely multiple solutions to a certain problem can be a significant mental shift in problem solving (especially for problems we are familiar with). With this new mindset, we embrace the freedom to design many solutions and select the most appropriate for the problem at hand.

In the parable, the problem is that children are drowning in the river. Under pressure to save the children, the rescuers repeatedly implement the most obvious solution. Only when one rescuer thinks to focus upstream does a probable lasting solution present itself.

Upstream thinking allows us to merge the design-thinking world with the problem-solving world to create multiple solutions for existing problems. Often, the farther upstream we go from the initial problem, the more solutions become obvious and available—and innovative. We find the freedom to design and implement a solution that is most likely to fully address the problem.

A great example of upstream thinking can be found in the use of metro turnstiles in Paris to create clean energy. Climate change is a pressing issue around the globe. With each year bringing more one-of-a-kind storms, wildfires, hurricanes, rising sea temperatures, and more, Paris began a groundbreaking project to harness novel green energy. In a *Medium* article, Eddie Tsui wrote: "As commuters pass through the turnstiles, their movements spin the turbines, generating kinetic energy. Though each rotation produces a small amount of energy, the cumulative effect is significant due to the millions of daily commuters using the metro system" (2023). This use of turnstiles in Paris might be the launching point for an innovative solution to tapping new sources of green energy. Imagine how much energy could be created from similar hotspots such as airports, railway stations, and office buildings. According to Tsui, "Initiatives that empower individuals to participate in the energy transition, even through daily activities, are vital in shaping a greener world" (2023).

Another excellent example of upstream thinking involves Dubai allowing its beaches to be used at night instead of during the swelteringly hot summer days. Due to extreme temperatures, the beaches in Dubai were growing increasingly less populated during the day. In an effort to "increase the city's quality of life," the government of Dubai decided to open the beaches at night (Nereim, 2023). Night beaches, with cooler temperatures, have become extremely popular, allowing people to enjoy the ocean without fear of deadly heat exhaustion or dehydration. Night beaches have become so popular that lifeguards work night shifts and large spotlights are used to provide light in the dark ocean.

This example of upstream thinking is not as far upstream as the Paris turnstiles but definitely offers an example of how designing solutions often requires us to shift our mindset of what we consider normal in order to create an innovative upstream solution.

Another solution highlighting our need to move farther upstream to create innovative ideas can be found in the company TranscribeGlass. TranscribeGlass was founded by two college students to provide an affordable artificial intelligence device that attaches to any pair of glasses to project real-time captions directly onto the lens of the glass (Duran, 2023). One of the creators uses the product himself because he has had "bilateral hearing loss since the age of three and uses hearing aids and lip reading to communicate" (Duran, 2023). The other creator was passionate about this problem after "learning that a Deaf friend had dropped out [of school] due to accessibility issues" (Duran, 2023). Several solutions already existed for this problem, but the two student creators felt the current solutions had not completely solved the problem. For example, hearing aids and cochlear implants do not work well for all users or in crowded areas. Other devices such as Google's Live Transcribe require users to look at another device to read the transcript, causing them to lose eye contact with the person talking (Duran, 2023).

When we look at upstream thinking in the field of education, creating innovative upstream ideas does not have to be complicated. One education example comes from DeJuan Strickland, a fourth-grade student who did not have money in his lunch account, and yet he had to sit in the cafeteria while his classmates ate lunch. This experience stayed with him (Reid, 2023). As a fourteen-year-old, his experience from elementary school was still prominent in his mind. He did not want other children to have the same experience, so he decided to do something about it. He started a GoFundMe with the goal of $400 to pay off the student lunch debt at his former elementary school. Strickland told a local reporter, "You should have free lunch everywhere, because kids need to eat. If I can't eat, then I can't work as efficiently as I'm supposed to; my body's not going to feel right" (Reid, 2023). His act of kindness became widely known and was celebrated in *Time* magazine, by Jennifer Hudson, and by others. He created Tech Boy Lunch Heroes, an initiative that creates accounts from which students can pay off negative school lunch balances. He has raised almost $10,000.

The issue of student lunch debt is prominent across the US, with annual student lunch debt totaling $262 million (Reid, 2023). DeJuan chose to solve the problem by paying off the lunch debt for students in his hometown. If we look at this issue further upstream, there are many other potential solutions that will create a larger impact, including creating initiatives like DeJuan's for every state or creating policies to eliminate the requirement to purchase lunch for all students.

Incredibly innovative upstream solutions exist in our world. Now that you know about upstream thinking, you will likely start to notice upstream solutions in your life.

BARRIERS TO UPSTREAM THINKING

In *Upstream*, Heath (2020) mentions a few barriers to the idea of upstream thinking. Unless you recognize and remove these barriers, your success in upstream thinking and problem solving will be affected. Two of the most common barriers mentioned in *Upstream* are problem blindness and lack of ownership (Heath, 2020).

PROBLEM BLINDNESS

One barrier to upstream thinking is problem blindness (Heath, 2020). Sometimes we fail to recognize problems, because we begin to think of them as part of our regular existence. This idea is called "inattentional blindness," meaning our "careful attention to one task leads us to miss important information that's unrelated to that task" (Heath, 2020). Problem blindness is essentially a "lack of peripheral vision" (Heath, 2020). Teachers working in secure schools struggle with problem blindness due to the constant chaos present inside the facilities. Part of this chaos results from two controlling entities with differing goals—the facility side and the education side. Because both sides have different missions and include fallible human beings, they do not always agree when making decisions. For example, students are often brought to school late in the mornings for various reasons, such as breakfast being late, showers taking too long, officers arriving late, and so on. Students arriving to class late or leaving early is a constant issue that teachers often ignore because it becomes normalized.

Heath suggests that "we grow accustomed to stimuli that are consistent" (2020). For example, you walk into a room and "notice the loud drone of an air conditioner, and five minutes later, the hum has receded into normalcy" (Heath, 2020). This normalcy often causes teachers in secure schools to ignore the late arrivals and constant interruptions, essentially functioning as if the problem does not exist. Instead, one solution is to purposefully plan activities at the beginning of class that can easily be removed if students arrive late. Like secure school teachers, you too may be blind to problems occurring every single day in your school, but once the problems have become part of your regular routine. To create effective solutions, we must remove the blinders and use our entire field of vision to see all existing problems.

> One teacher kept saying her students were constantly distracted in her classroom. Observing the class revealed the students were distracted because they were constantly using their phones. The teacher was blind to the problem of cell phone use because it had become a normal day-to-day occurrence—almost like missing exit signs on the highway because you see so many. The teacher implemented a policy in her classroom where phones could be used during class only with teacher permission. Removing the phones created a less distracting environment for students.

LACK OF OWNERSHIP

The second barrier to upstream thinking is a lack of problem ownership (Heath, 2020). Problems often continue to exist simply because no one takes ownership of them. People affected by the problem ask, "Can someone fix this problem?" If everyone affected by the problem is hoping someone else will implement a solution, then no one is actually working to solve the problem. In secure schools, students attend school with their living pod. Living pods are designed based on safety and security protocols, not necessarily grade levels. Attending school with a living pod means a single class may consist of four different grade levels or three different subject areas at once. Multi-level teaching is a major issue in secure schools, and teachers feel they cannot create a solution because they do not determine where students are housed. Lack of problem ownership essentially means that no one is solving the problem. While teachers cannot force the facility to house students in similar grades or ages together, they can structure their classroom in a way that benefits all students.

Another major issue in secure schools involves students arriving late to class due to officers bringing them late. While teachers cannot force officers to bring students on time, they can design a solution to implement within their classroom and own the problem from within their sphere of control. Teachers can purposefully design every minute of class time and place activities at the beginning of class that if completed add to the lesson overall. If not completed because students are late, the activities can easily be left off the agenda. Controlling the beginning of the class period allows teachers to own the problem and implement a successful solution. Problems likely persist in your school or classroom because no one is taking ownership. Before we can create and implement effective solutions, we must understand which problems are within our sphere of control.

Once we remove the barriers of problem blindness and lack of ownership, we can truthfully acknowledge all current problems and take ownership of those problems.

> At one school, teachers felt pressured to never take a day off, because they did not have many substitutes to cover classes, and creating a last-minute sub plan was exhausting. The teachers felt that this problem was beyond their sphere of control. Realizing this was an issue, the administrator created a sub-folder policy where each teacher kept a physical folder in the office that contained their schedule, class lists, notes, and a QR code. The QR code linked to a Google Doc where teachers would place specific plans for the day they would be out. While implementing this new sub-folder plan did not increase the number of subs available, it did make covering classes easier for colleagues and lowered the amount of stress on the teacher taking a personal day, because the teacher did not have to update the physical folder, only the Google Doc. The administrator took ownership of this problem and lowered the stress of teachers taking personal days.

SELECTING THE RIGHT PROBLEM

Problems can be personal and subjective. A problem for me might not be a problem for you, and vice versa. Problems can exist in every area of your life—your classroom, school, home, and family. Problems exist all around us and can be overwhelming. With a mindset geared toward designing upstream solutions, these problems can be addressed, but we must decide where to begin. When selecting a problem to solve, the best place to begin is to understand the impact of the problem and the level of influence you have over the problem area.

IMPACT

Understanding the impact of various problems is crucial to deciding which problem should be addressed first. Some problems are low on the overall impact scale, and others are high. It's best to address problems on the higher end of the impact scale, because the higher the problem is on the impact scale, the more people the problem affects (**Figure 2.1**). For example, arriving late to school every day is a low impact problem. It might be extremely frustrating and impactful for the teacher or administrator arriving late, but it does not affect many others. In contrast, a school deciding to implement a brand-new curriculum in every subject area is an example of a high-impact problem. This problem affects every teacher, student, and parent at the school. While solving the low-impact problem of tardiness is important, solving the high-impact curriculum problem affecting the entire school should be higher on the priority list. This does not mean the tardiness problem should not be solved, it simply means it should be placed on hold while problems that have a greater impact take priority.

LESS   LEVEL OF IMPACT   MORE

FIGURE 2.1 A visual graph representing the impact scale.

INFLUENCE

Another crucial aspect when selecting a problem is understanding how much influence you have over the problem area. Using the previous examples, a classroom teacher has great influence over arrival time but very little influence over the choice of curriculum used by the school. However, an administrator has great influence over the curriculum used but perhaps not much influence over one teacher's arrival time. The most frustrating part of problem solving is trying to solve problems outside our realm of influence. There are many ways to look at influence. In Chapter 4, we will focus on the influence we have over potential solutions. Right now, we must consider the level of influence we have over problems (**Figure 2.2**). Classroom teachers and administrators are told *what* to teach—specific units, subject areas, professional development topics, and so on. *How* we choose to cover the units or provide the required professional development is often within our influence. Understanding how much influence you have over a problem is a pivotal first step in selecting the right problem. If you select a problem outside your realm of influence, you lower the probability that you will be able to implement a successful solution.

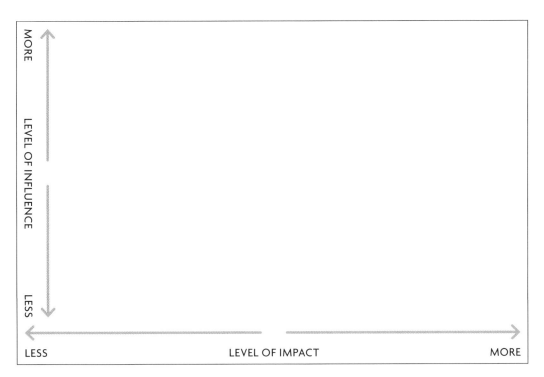

FIGURE 2.2 Graph potential problems according to level of impact and level of influence.

In the workbook section of this chapter, you will select one specific problem and then design and implement a solution for that problem as you continue through this book. You can choose a problem in any area of your life. However, you should choose a problem that has a high impact and that falls well within your sphere of influence.

🔔 FIRE DRILL!

Welcome to your next Fire Drill! You can now put into practice what you've learned throughout this chapter by using the impact and influence scale to select the most appropriate problem. Scan the QR code to hear more detailed information from the author about the activities in this section.

**kaylahholland.com/
puttingoutfires/audio**

IQUADRANT

As we learned in this chapter, the first and most crucial steps in selecting a problem to address are to determine the current problems you are facing, understand the varying impact of those problems, and understand your varying influence over the problem areas.

1. Set a timer for ten minutes, and write down as many problems as you can think of in the space provided below. Do not think about potential solutions just yet. This exercise is designed to uncover all the problems you are facing, including those that you might be blind to seeing, and those you do not think you have ownership of.

_____

_____

_____

_____

_____

_____

2. Once you create the list of problems, use the IQuadrants graph below to place each individual problem in the correct spot according to its level of impact and your influence over it. Your goal is to select a problem in the upper right corner.

Problems in the upper left corner are well within your influence but do not impact many people. These problems can be placed on the back burner for now. Problems in the lower left corner are low-impact problems you have little influence over. You would need an ally that has more influence in this area to implement a successful solution, and any solution would have minimal impact. Problems in the lower right corner affect many people, but fall outside your sphere of influence, so again, a strategic ally would be needed. The upper right corner is your sweet spot! These are high-impact problems that you have great influence over. Select one of these problems to address as you complete this book.

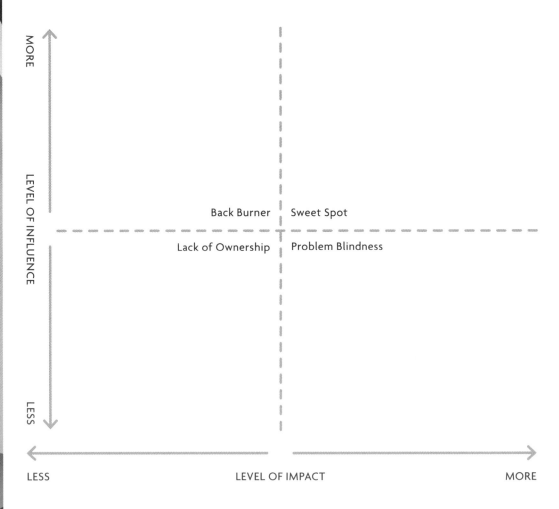

MORE

LEVEL OF INFLUENCE

LESS

Back Burner | Sweet Spot

Lack of Ownership | Problem Blindness

LESS   LEVEL OF IMPACT   MORE

ROOT CAUSE

Using your selected problem, complete the activity below to find the root cause of the problem. In this activity you will ask the question *Why?* five times. Asking why repeatedly helps determine the true cause of a problem. We often see the symptoms and fail to fully understand the true cause. Begin by describing the problem and ask your first *why*. Write your answer in the space provided, and ask *why* again. Continue this process until you have asked *why* five times and have determined the root cause. Write it in the space provided. Space is also provided for you to write any takeaways you obtain from this experience (Bolger, 2022).

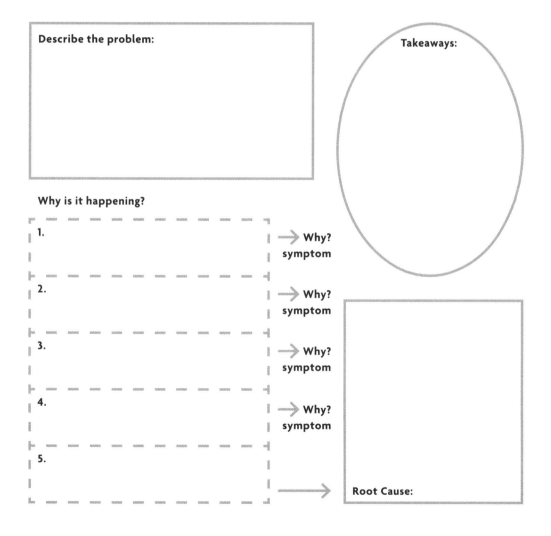

Describe the problem:

Takeaways:

Why is it happening?

1.
→ Why? symptom

2.
→ Why? symptom

3.
→ Why? symptom

4.
→ Why? symptom

5.

Root Cause:

SAMPLE PROBLEMS

As discussed in Chapter 1, these sample problems are meant to act as a guide and highlight how the activities in each Fire Drill! section should be completed.

TEACHER: PURPOSEFUL TECHNOLOGY USE TO ENHANCE STUDENT LEARNING

A teacher has numerous problems as shown in the list below.

Teacher's Problem List

- Trying to keep up with technology trends while teaching a full curriculum

- Creating clear classroom digital use policies

- Developing equitable assessment methods that are fair and unbiased

- Using technology with purpose to enhance student learning

- Assessing high-quality digital resources

- Navigating technical issues

- Some students do not have access to technology at home

- Navigating copyright and fair use regulations when using digital content in the classroom

- Engaging parents in the technology integration process

- Creating digital policies that are fair and address issues responsibly

- Teaching students how to use technology responsibly

- Resolving my own fear of technology and using it in the classroom

- Keeping students from becoming distracted while using technology

- Maintaining classroom discipline while using technology

When completing the IQuadrants activity, the teacher was able to categorize the problems according to levels of impact and influence. The selected problem, found in the sweet spot, is *using technology with purpose to enhance student learning.*

Teacher's IQuadrant

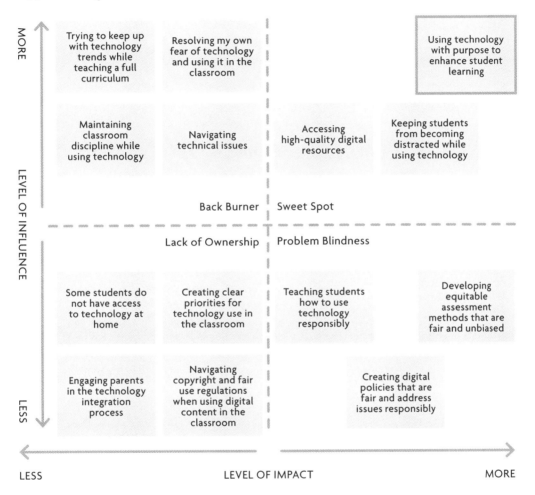

MORE

Trying to keep up with technology trends while teaching a full curriculum

Resolving my own fear of technology and using it in the classroom

Using technology with purpose to enhance student learning

Maintaining classroom discipline while using technology

Navigating technical issues

Accessing high-quality digital resources

Keeping students from becoming distracted while using technology

LEVEL OF INFLUENCE

Back Burner | Sweet Spot

Lack of Ownership | Problem Blindness

Some students do not have access to technology at home

Creating clear priorities for technology use in the classroom

Teaching students how to use technology responsibly

Developing equitable assessment methods that are fair and unbiased

Engaging parents in the technology integration process

Navigating copyright and fair use regulations when using digital content in the classroom

Creating digital policies that are fair and address issues responsibly

LESS

LESS   LEVEL OF IMPACT   MORE

When completing the Root Cause activity, the teacher realized the root of the technology issue can actually be described as *a lack of personalized learning.*

Teacher's Root Cause

Describe the problem: Using technology seamlessly in the classroom is important because we need to equip students with skills like digital literacy, critical thinking, and problem-solving. It helps to engage students in experiences taking place in the classroom.

Takeaway:
The issue of student engagement can be addressed by designing personalized learning experiences.

Why is it happening?

1. Students are often bored in my classroom, leading to behavioral and classroom management issues.

   → **Why?** **symptom**

2. They are not engaged in the content being taught.

   → **Why?** **symptom**

3. The content does not always address their interests, needs, or abilities.

   → **Why?** **symptom**

4. It is difficult to design engaging experiences that meet the needs of all my learners.

   → **Why?** **symptom**

5. Students need me to design personalized learning paths that address their interests, needs, and abilities.

   →

Root Cause: Students are not engaged in my lessons because the content taught in my classroom is not relevant and meaningful and does not meet the individual needs, interests, and abilities of all my students.

ISTE Standards: For Educators

2.5a: Use technology to create, adapt and personalize learning experiences that foster independent learning and accommodate learner differences and needs (ISTE, 2017).

2.6d: Model and nurture creativity and creative expression to communicate ideas, knowledge or connections (ISTE, 2017).

ADMINISTRATOR: ENSURING SCHOOLWIDE TECHNOLOGY PROGRAMS MEET THE NEEDS OF DIVERSE LEARNERS

An administrator has numerous problems as shown in the problem list activity below, and these problems are vastly different from those of a teacher.

Administrator's Problem List

- Ensuring all students have equitable access to technology and the internet—even at home

- Addressing gaps in digital literacy skills among students

- Ensuring schoolwide technology problems meet the needs of diverse learners

- Accessing adaptive learning tools and strategies to help students with disabilities

- Creating digital policies that are fair and address issues responsibly

- Balancing the current budget to ensure technology remains up to date

- Aligning technology use with curriculum standards

- Addressing parent/guardian concerns about the impact of technology on students

- Providing effective professional development for teachers

- Including culturally relevant materials and addressing language barriers

- Creating policies that promote equitable access to digital tools and resources

- Developing equitable assessment methods that are fair and unbiased

- Protecting students and teachers from cybersecurity threats

- Creating programs to teach students about responsible and ethical technology use

When completing the IQuadrants activity, the administrator was able to categorize the problems to determine the level of impact and influence. The selected problem is found in the sweet spot and is *ensuring schoolwide technology programs meet the needs of diverse learners.*

Administrator's IQuadrant

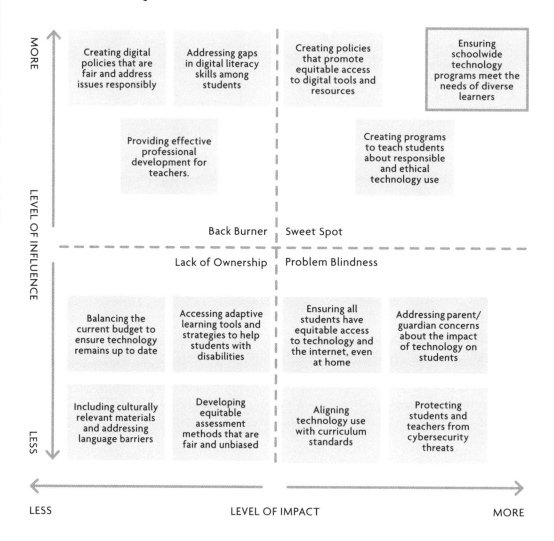

CHAPTER 2: WHAT'S YOUR PROBLEM?

When completing the Root Cause activity, the administrator realizes the technology issue can actually be described as a staff issue.

Administrator's Root Cause

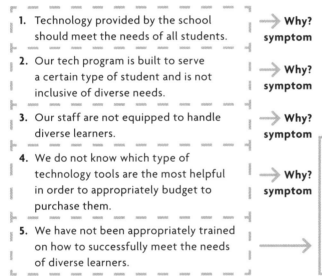

Describe the problem: Meeting the needs of diverse learners includes adaptive learning tools, language barriers, and restructuring policies to be less punitive and is important because we need to ensure the technology provided at school removes obstacles to helping students' success instead of creating obstacles.

Takeaway:
The issue of meeting the needs of diverse learners is not a technology issue but a staff knowledge issue.

Why is it happening?

1. Technology provided by the school should meet the needs of all students. → **Why? symptom**

2. Our tech program is built to serve a certain type of student and is not inclusive of diverse needs. → **Why? symptom**

3. Our staff are not equipped to handle diverse learners. → **Why? symptom**

4. We do not know which type of technology tools are the most helpful in order to appropriately budget to purchase them. → **Why? symptom**

5. We have not been appropriately trained on how to successfully meet the needs of diverse learners. →

Root Cause: The needs of diverse learners are not being met by our technology program because we do not know which types of digital programs are most successful and without knowing that we cannot budget for them to be purchased.

 ISTE Standards: for Education Leaders

3.1b: Ensure all students have access to the technology and connectivity necessary to participate in authentic and engaging learning opportunities (ISTE, 2018).

3.3d: Support educators in using technology to advance learning that meets the diverse learning, cultural, and social-emotional needs of individual students (ISTE, 2018).

WHAT HAPPENS NEXT?

You now understand the impact and influence of your problems, have selected a problem, and determined the root cause of that problem. In the next chapter, we will look more closely at the people involved in your problem area.

The smoke is rising. Let's march bravely into the next chapter and learn about the people involved in the problem before implementing our firefighting skills.

CHAPTER 3
PEOPLE AT THE CENTER

THE BEAUTIFUL THING ABOUT DESIGN THINKING is that there is often not a single specific answer, and that can lead to more questions. With upstream thinking, there may be multiple solutions to one problem. We completed numerous activities in Chapter 2 that help us understand the problem more deeply. Despite the ambiguous and creative nature of this process, one fundamental truth remains: people are at the center of it all. Your focus must remain on the people directly impacted by the problem. When solving problems, it is easy to get so lost in the issues or the potential solutions that we forget about the actual people we began designing solutions for in the first place. By placing these people at the center of our process, we gain insight into their needs, wants, dreams, and goals. We learn to listen with curious minds and think first with empathy, placing our own views of the world aside to better understand the perspective of another person.

Ela Ben-Ur created a framework to remind us of the importance of keeping people at the center when problem solving. Her framework is called Innovators' Compass (**Figure 3.1**), and it literally keeps people at the center (Ben-Ur, 2020). Using a compass as the design is an excellent visual, because a compass represents a journey. This process of blending design-thinking practices with the idea of upstream thinking and merging it into the *Putting Out Fires* Framework is just that, a journey. The journey can be long and arduous, but it can also be extremely enjoyable and rewarding. We journey through a fascinating realm where empathy, creativity, and problem-solving converge to shape the world around us. However, it will not be as rewarding or enjoyable, meaning we will not create a successful solution if we lose sight of the main goal—keeping people at the center.

When we keep people at the center, we essentially design for belonging. Isn't belonging what we all want—to feel loved, welcomed, and valued? The feeling of belonging allows us to be brave and take risks. Susie Wise in *Design for Belonging* writes that "belonging is a real factor in having the confidence to believe in oneself and in one's ability to do hard things" (2022, p. 19). Designing our solutions with people at the center helps us create a sense of belonging for everyone impacted by the problem. Designing for belonging in school settings also improves educational outcomes, because when students have a sense of belonging they "interpret setbacks and difficulty in their studies as a normal part of learning, rather than signs they are 'out of place'" (Wise, 2022, p. 19). Research also shows that improving educational outcomes affects the personal lives of students by improving their "health, wealth, and connectedness" as adults; therefore, designing for belonging leads to success for students in school and life (Wise, 2022, p. 19).

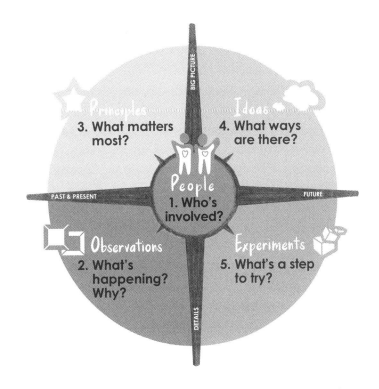

In *Upstream*, Heath discusses how we must consider each potential solution's impact so that we do not cause more harm than the initial problem (2020). In fact, we need to look at all the vantage points of those impacted by the problem to see how the problem and potential solutions affect everyone involved. Heath writes that in looking at the problem and potential solutions, we must ask ourselves, "What are the second-order effects of our efforts: If we try to eliminate X . . . what will fill the void? If we invest more time and energy in a particular problem, what will receive less focus as a result, and how might that inattention affect the system as a whole?" (2020, p. 176). If we fail to see all aspects of the problem and potential solution, we run the risk of doing more harm than good in solving the problem.

To better understand this concept, let's consider the solution implemented for the problem of low-performing schools in Houston, Texas. In the spring of 2023, the state of Texas took control over the Houston Independent School District (HISD) due in part to low-performing schools (Goodman, 2023). The newly elected superintendent, Mike Miles, with no educational experience in his background, began to implement a new plan for HISD (Goodman, 2023). One component of this new plan was to transition libraries into other roles, including isolating students removed from class due to behavior issues so they could join lessons virtually. Even though low reading levels are prominent across

HISD, over two dozen elementary and middle school libraries were closed and transitioned to a "team center," where students were sent as a disciplinary action (Adams, 2022). This is a classic example of a solution being implemented without fully understanding the causes behind the problem itself, and it did more harm than good. This solution greatly affected low-performing students, because they are the ones typically disrupting class with negative behaviors. Many behavior issues take place in the classroom because students are unengaged in the lesson. Some reasons include because they do not understand the content; because they need to be challenged with extended learning opportunities; because they are distracted with personal, often traumatic, events at home; or because they do not feel they are in a safe environment. Instead of doing the hard work to better understand the problem causing the low-performing schools, the solution of removing disruptive students was implemented, causing harm to all students due to the lack of libraries. No library access caused an even greater increase in low reading levels. Students sent to these "team centers" do not feel welcome or valued. They feel out of place and unwanted, and their grades suffer, because instead of receiving direct instruction and supplemental support from the classroom teacher, they sit in a room alone.

When we fail to keep people at the center of the solutions designed, we inevitably cause more harm than intended.

KEEP PEOPLE AT THE CENTER

Who, then, is impacted by your specific problem? An important step in problem solving is to determine every single person that is affected by the problem you selected. I suggest calling the people affected by your selected problem "clients" to help remind you that you are designing for them. Clients can include students, teachers, administrators, parents, members of the community, and others. It is important to understand how the problem is affecting each type of client. The best way to do that is to literally put yourself in their shoes. Live their life for a day, metaphorically. Once you see the problem from their perspective, it will be much easier to design a creative solution with their best interests in mind.

The *Putting Out Fires* Framework is fundamentally about creating solutions for people. Whether your final solution requires designing a product, implementing an idea, altering your teaching style, updating policies, or completely changing an entire school system, the ultimate success of the solution is determined by how well it meets the needs and preferences of the people impacted by it.

🔔 FIRE DRILL!

Welcome to your third Fire Drill! You can now put into practice what you've learned throughout this chapter, including the importance of keeping people at the center and ensuring your solution will not do more harm than good. Scan the QR code to hear more detailed information from the author about the activities in this section.

kaylahholland.com/ puttingoutfires/audio

DETERMINE WHO YOUR PEOPLE ARE

To determine the people affected by your problem, begin by listing people in the far-left column below. In the middle column list any assumptions you are making about those people, and in the far-right column, list questions you have for those people. You can list specific people (e.g., your principal or superintendent) or general groups of people (e.g., students, teachers, or parents) (Greenberg et al., 2021, p. 146). Remember that it is important to think of these people as your clients because you are designing solutions for them.

PEOPLE	ASSUMPTIONS	QUESTIONS

EMPATHY MAP

In this activity, select a person from the list of people you just created. If selecting a group of people—for example, students—imagine one specific student (real or fictional). To better understand your selected person, write in the spaces below what this person might think, feel, say, and do when impacted by your selected problem (Lewrick et al., 2020, p. 93).

For a deeper dive, complete this step for every person (or group) that you listed.

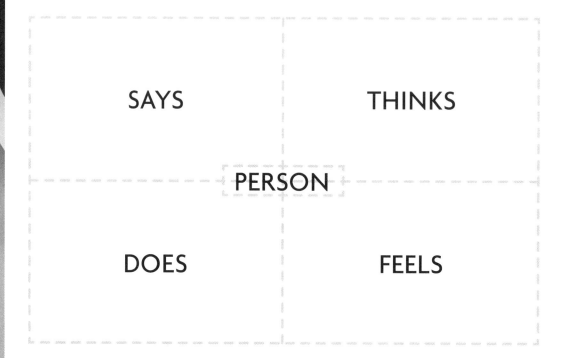

HOW MIGHT WE . . .

In this activity, you will create a *how might we* statement to design a question using specific language. Fill in the blanks below to construct the *how might we* statement (Lewrick et al., 2020, p. 125).

1. Write a word in the *action* blank that describes what you would like to take place. For example: change, improve, or recreate.

2. Describe the problem as a phrase in the *what* blank. For example: active learning experiences, best practices for implementing technology in education, etc.

3. List the people impacted by the problem in the *who* blank. For example: students, teachers.

4. Describe the end result you are hoping to achieve in the *change* blank.

How might we action _____

what _____

for who _____

to change _____

SAMPLE PROBLEMS

Let's check in with our sample problems introduced in Chapter 2. How did the teacher and administrator complete the activities in the Fire Drill! section for this chapter?

TEACHER: PURPOSEFUL TECHNOLOGY USE TO ENHANCE STUDENT LEARNING

The teacher created a list of the people impacted by the chosen problem and determined the assumptions and questions for a specific group or individual, such as: "Do students really not care about their academics, or am I not creating an engaging experience?" or "Am I really too busy to try something new, or am I actually just afraid I will make a mistake?"

Teacher's People List

PEOPLE	ASSUMPTIONS	QUESTIONS
Students	Students don't care about their academics.	How do I enhance student engagement?
Teachers	Other teachers use the same content I do.	Which teacher do students enjoy learning from the most?
Parents	Parents only care about grades.	Would parents care if I did not have as many grades per quarter?
Principals	My principal will not like me trying new things.	Can I ask the principal for professional development on this topic?
Me	I'm too busy to learn new ways of teaching.	Am I too busy or simply afraid?
Tech Coaches	The tech coach is too busy to help me.	Is the tech coach too busy or am I afraid of asking her?

The sample empathy map below allowed the teacher to view the perspective of a student. The student might be saying, "I'm bored," but might actually be feeling overwhelmed, causing them to act out in class.

Teacher's Empathy Map

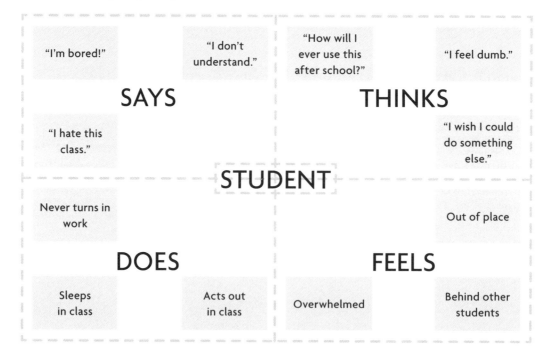

Once the teacher better understood the perspective of the student, the teacher created a *how might we* statement using specific language to create a question that deserves to be answered. The *how might we* statement created was: "How might we improve classroom instruction for students to engage them in lessons that are relevant and meaningful?"

Teacher's How Might We...

How might we <u>improve</u>

classroom instruction

for <u>students</u>

to <u>engage them in lessons that are relevant and useful?</u>

 ISTE Standards: For Educators

2.3b: Establish a learning culture that promotes curiosity and critical examination of online resources and fosters digital literacy and media fluency (ISTE, 2017).

2.7c: Use assessment data to guide progress and communicate with students, parents and education stakeholders to build student self-direction (ISTE, 2017).

ADMINISTRATOR: ENSURING SCHOOLWIDE TECHNOLOGY PROGRAMS MEET THE NEEDS OF DIVERSE LEARNERS

The administrator created a list of the people involved and determined the assumptions and questions for a specific individual or group, such as: "Do students really not care about school, or are we not creating a safe environment?"

Administrator's People List

PEOPLE	ASSUMPTIONS	QUESTIONS
Students	Students don't care about school.	Are we making sure students feel that school is a safe place to be themselves?
Teachers	Teachers do not want one more thing.	How are teachers currently meeting the needs of their students?
Parents	Parents only care about grades.	Would parents care if students were given different assignments?
Special Education Coordinators	Special education coordinators are overwhelmed.	What do special education coordinators think about our current gaps in meeting the needs of diverse learners?
Me	I'm too busy to implement this type of change.	Am I too busy or simply afraid?
Tech Coaches	The tech coach is too busy to create a new plan for all types of learners.	What does the tech coach think about our current gaps in meeting the needs of diverse learners?

The sample empathy map allowed the administrator to view the perspective of a student. The student might be saying, "I hate this class," but might actually be feeling out of place, causing them to make fun of others.

Administrator's Empathy Map

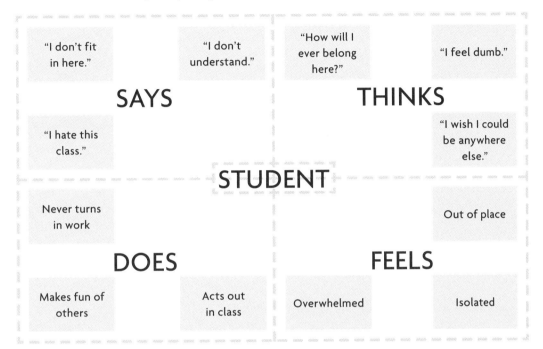

"I don't fit in here."

"I don't understand."

"How will I ever belong here?"

"I feel dumb."

SAYS

THINKS

"I hate this class."

"I wish I could be anywhere else."

STUDENT

Never turns in work

Out of place

DOES

FEELS

Makes fun of others

Acts out in class

Overwhelmed

Isolated

Once the administrator better understood the perspective of the student, they created a *how might we* statement using specific language to create a question that deserves to be answered. The *how might we* statement created was: "How might we improve digital programming for all students to meet the diverse needs that currently exist?"

Administrator's How Might We...

How might we improve

digital programming

for all students

to meet the diverse needs that currently exist?

 ISTE Standards: For Education Leaders

3.3c: Inspire a culture of innovation and collaboration that allows the time and space to explore and experiment with digital tools (ISTE, 2018).

3.5d: Develop the skills needed to lead and navigate change, advance systems and promote a mindset of continuous improvement for how technology can improve learning (ISTE, 2018).

WHAT HAPPENS NEXT?

In this chapter, you selected a problem, completed activities to better understand the problem, and kept people at the center of your potential solution. As we learned with upstream thinking in Chapter 2, many problems have numerous possible solutions, so let's explore all the ways you can put out the fire in the next chapter.

CHAPTER 4
THE PUTTING OUT FIRES FRAMEWORK

IN THE WORLD OF EDUCATION, we are actively involved in solving problems every day. Some problems warrant quick solutions, while others require us to go through a design process to identify multiple creative solutions. Educators are putting out fires every single day. Putting out fires day after day feels so natural that we often resemble the people from the river parable in Chapter 2.

To break this cycle, I created the *Putting Out Fires* Framework (**Figure 4.1**) to help educators solve problems—and additionally to help them categorize potential solutions so that the best solution can be implemented. Design thinking and upstream thinking offer excellent strategies for problem categorization and selection, but fall short once potential solutions are identified, often leaving us with numerous solutions and no further strategy for judging the merits of the solutions we have identified.

Prevent	**Contain**	**Detect**	**Extinguish**
The problem has been eliminated but the solution involves time, resources, and people.	The problem has been confined to a small space, limiting harm, while it is studied.	The problem has been analyzed by looking directly at the symptoms involved.	The problem is quickly assessed and addressed but will likely return.

FIGURE 4.1 The *Putting Out Fires* Framework.

The *Putting Out Fires* Framework helps to categorize solutions so that we may select the most appropriate solution for the problem. The four categories of the *Putting Out Fires* Framework echo the four fire-prevention categories: prevent, detect, contain, and extinguish (International Fire Safety Standards Coalition, 2020). The *Putting Out Fires* Framework aligns these four fire-prevention strategies with different types of solutions, to aid in the selection of the most appropriate solution.

- A solution in the **Extinguish** category quickly assesses and addresses the problem, but the solution applied does not address the root of the problem, so the problem will likely reoccur.

- A solution in the **Detect** category reflects time spent analyzing the symptoms and root of the problem before implementation.

- A solution in the **Contain** category confines the problem to a small space where the causes can be further studied, limiting the harm caused.

- A solution in the **Prevent** category eliminates the problem permanently but involves time, resources, and people.

Let's view the parable from Chapter 2 according to the *Putting Out Fires* Framework. Multiple solutions could address the issue of children drowning in the river. At first, the people in the parable were stuck in their cycle of response, and the problem kept reoccurring, which fits nicely into the Extinguish category. A solution in the Detect category might be to provide life preservers and make lifeguards available, which would allow time to research the problem in hopes of identifying a better solution later. A solution in the Contain category might be to teach kids to swim, so they avoid drowning altogether, which would contain the problem entirely no matter what body of water kids might encounter. A solution in the Prevent category might be to drain the river, so kids simply cannot drown in that particular river, but this solution would require a good deal of time, resources, and people to implement.

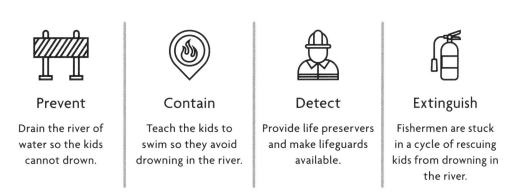

Prevent	Contain	Detect	Extinguish
Drain the river of water so the kids cannot drown.	Teach the kids to swim so they avoid drowning in the river.	Provide life preservers and make lifeguards available.	Fishermen are stuck in a cycle of rescuing kids from drowning in the river.

FIGURE 4.2 The parable from Chapter 2 viewed according to the *Putting Out Fires* Framework.

Most of these solutions are practical and doable, although draining the river would likely create a whole host of other problems. The framework helps us assess all potential solutions in the various categories before selecting the best solution possible. In this scenario, the most appropriate solution is in the Contain category, where we teach kids to swim so they avoid drowning in all bodies of water, not just in the river. However, it might be important to begin with the Detect solution of providing lifeguards on the river while kids are being taught to swim.

This is a very simplistic example of the *Putting Out Fires* Framework. In future chapters, we will consider each of these categories in more detail. To start, let's identify many potential solutions for your chosen problem area so that we can organize the solutions using the four categories. However, before we jump into organizing solutions, we need to identify them, and before we identify them, we need to understand our own levels of capacity and influence over potential solutions.

LEVELS OF CAPACITY AND INFLUENCE

Many factors will influence your choice of the best solution to a problem. The two most important factors are the levels of capacity and influence you have over both the problem area and potential solutions.

Consider the following questions to determine your capacity when it comes to the problem and potential solutions. We will look further into this concept in the Fire Drill! section of this chapter.

Ask yourself the following: To support a given solution,

- Do you have the people needed?
- Do you have funds available?
- Do you have the necessary supplies?
- Do you have the time?
- Do you have the physical space?
- Do you have the mental space?
- Do you have the policies needed?
- Do you have support from your team and/or leadership?

You may be asking yourself, what if I don't have capacity in many of these areas? Maybe your grant application was not approved, or your administration is not supportive. You can still effect change in your classroom or school without meeting all of the capacity considerations.

Every person has a circle of influence. In the Fire Drill! section of this chapter, you will complete an activity involving two circles (inner and outer). Items that are within the inner circle are within our realm of influence. For example, as a teacher, you have major influence over your classroom, because even if you do not determine the content or policies, you still decide how the content is taught or how discipline is delivered. For example, you might choose to have restorative practices instead of punitive discipline. As an administrator, you decide how the budget is spent and what professional development will be offered throughout the year. These are all items within our realm of influence. Items in the outer circle are things we cannot influence. For example, a teacher does not decide how the annual budget is spent, and an administrator cannot control how a teacher presents content.

Trying to implement solutions outside of our realm of influence and level of capacity will likely be frustrating, exhausting, and ultimately unsuccessful. Of course, we can work toward gaining allies who have influence where we need it, but that step needs to be taken before tackling problems outside of our influence.

You *can* effect change and implement a potential solution. You simply need to be realistic about your capacity and influence. If you do not have access to funds, do not select a solution that requires a hefty purchase. If you do not have the support of administrators, do not select a solution that requires a major overhaul of policies and procedures. Remember, there are numerous solutions to every problem. Putting a solution in place that honors your capacity and is within your realm of influence might open more avenues and resources for you later, once your solution shows results.

FIRE DRILL!

Welcome to your next Fire Drill! You can now put into practice what you've learned throughout this chapter, including using the *Putting Out Fires* Framework to categorize potential solutions, considering your capacity, and determining your realm of influence. Scan the QR code to hear more detailed information from the author about the activities in this section.

kaylahholland.com/ puttingoutfires/audio

ONE HUNDRED IDEAS

It is now time to create potential solutions! This activity is challenging because we typically think of perhaps up to three solutions, but coming up with one hundred seems difficult. Completing this activity will stretch your brain to consider many options.

1. Grab a timer and set it to fifteen minutes.

2. Begin making a list of potential solutions in the spaces provided. Write down anything that comes to mind! Be creative, dream big, and do not worry about being realistic. The goal is to have as many potential solutions as possible.

3. When the timer ends, see how many solutions you have. (Don't worry if you didn't make it to one hundred.) Go through the list and place a star next to the solutions you think have the most potential (Bolger, 2022).

> If you are struggling with creating lots of potential solutions, you can try the following two ways to move your brainstorming activity forward. First, you can take your problem to a group of trusted people and complete the activity together. Second, you can use artificial intelligence to ask for solutions using something like the following prompt: "List 20 solutions for [insert your specific problem]".

CAPACITY CONSIDERATIONS

Use the activity below to evaluate how much capacity you would need to carry out your potential solutions. Choose two solutions and map out your capacity using the prompts in the boxes. Use two different colored pens to separate the two solutions. Consider both your personal capacity and the capacity of your school or district. For example, your own personal capacity should be considered for the prompts of time and mental space. However, you should consider the capacity of your school or district for prompts such as funding, physical space, and people. Some solutions may automatically be excluded because you simply do not have the capacity to see them through to the end. Other solutions might be so powerful that you decide to create capacity to make it happen.

Capacity Considerations

Time	Physical Space	Policy	Support	Mental Space	Supplies	Funds

Level of Capacity

LOTS OF CAPACITY	
SOME CAPACITY	
NO CAPACITY	

LEVEL OF INFLUENCE

Once you realize your capacity for individual solutions, you then need to determine your realm of influence. Fill in the circles below with items that are under your influence and those that are beyond your influence (Schaffner, 2023).

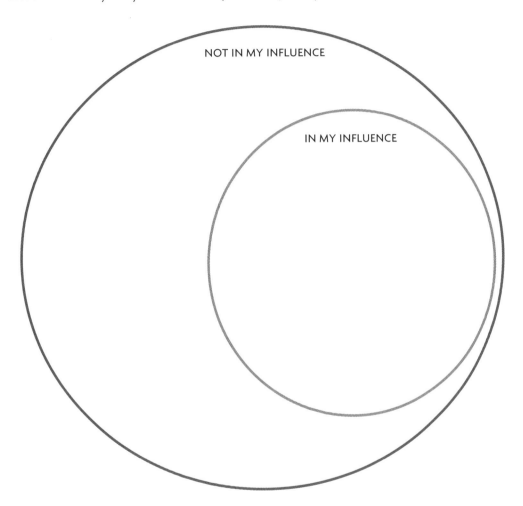

NOT IN MY INFLUENCE

IN MY INFLUENCE

SAMPLE PROBLEMS

Let's check in with the sample problems introduced in Chapter 2. How did the teacher and administrator complete the activities in the Fire Drill! section for this chapter?

TEACHER: PURPOSEFUL TECHNOLOGY USE TO ENHANCE STUDENT LEARNING

The teacher created more than twenty potential solutions to the problem of using technology to enhance student learning.

Teacher's One Hundred Ideas

Conduct regular workshops and training sessions to educate teachers about effective and purposeful use of technology in the classroom.	Create online repositories of educational technology tools, lesson plans, and resources for teachers to access and implement in their classrooms.	Encourage experienced teachers to mentor their peers, sharing successful strategies for integrating technology effectively.	Implement interactive online platforms that allow students to engage with educational content in a dynamic and personalized manner.	Develop educational apps that cater to various subjects, enabling students to learn at their own pace and according to their own style.
Introduce digital assessment tools that provide instant feedback to both students and teachers, facilitating a more responsive learning environment.	Encourage the flipped classroom approach, where students engage with digital content at home and utilize classroom time for discussions and collaborative activities.	Utilize AR and VR technologies to create immersive learning experiences, allowing students to explore complex concepts in a realistic environment.	Integrate educational games and gamified elements into the curriculum, making learning more engaging and interactive for students.	Organize podcasts and webinars with industry experts, giving students access to real-world insights and experiences.
Foster creativity by encouraging students to create digital stories, videos, and presentations to demonstrate their understanding of various subjects.	Facilitate collaborative projects that require students to work together online, promoting teamwork and digital communication skills.	Use cloud-based tools for document collaboration, allowing students and teachers to access and work on assignments from any device with an internet connection.	Leverage social media platforms to create educational communities, where students can discuss topics, share resources, and collaborate on projects.	Provide access to online tutorials and instructional videos that support classroom learning and cater to different learning styles.
Integrate lessons on digital ethics, online safety, and responsible internet use to promote good digital citizenship among students.	Establish a support hotline or chat service where teachers can seek immediate assistance with technology-related issues.	Ensure that all devices and software used in classrooms are up to date, providing a seamless user experience for both teachers and students.	Educate parents about the educational benefits of technology and involve them in their child's digital learning journey.	Advocate for universal internet access, ensuring that all students have equal opportunities to benefit from online resources.
Implement adaptive learning systems that assess students' abilities and tailor educational content to meet their specific needs and learning pace.	Collaborate with technology companies to provide schools with discounted or free access to educational software and hardware.	Use data analytics to track students' progress and identify areas where technology integration has been particularly effective or needs improvement.	Foster communities of practice where teachers can share their experiences, challenges, and successes related to technology integration	Invest in research to continuously evaluate the impact of technology on student learning, adapting strategies based on evidence-based practices.

The teacher then considered their capacity for two of the solutions. As you can see, this teacher has different types of capacity based on which solution is being mapped, but has no capacity for either solution in the categories of supplies, funds, or creating policies. Therefore, the teacher should not select a solution that requires any of those three categories. The teacher then determines what they can and cannot influence.

Teacher's Capacity Considerations

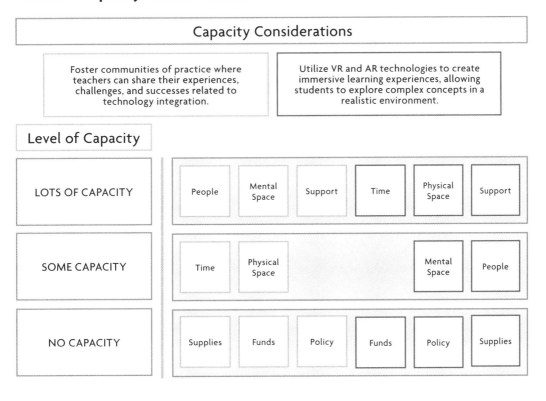

Teacher's Level of Influence

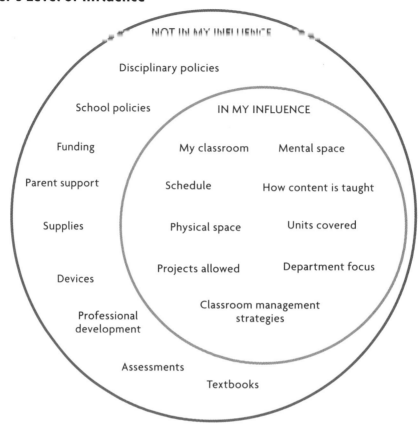

 ISTE Standards: For Educators

2.5b: Design authentic learning activities that align with content area standards and use digital tools and resources to maximize active, deep learning. (ISTE, 2017).

2.5c: Explore and apply instructional design principles to create innovative digital learning environments that engage and support learning (ISTE, 2017).

ADMINISTRATOR: ENSURING SCHOOLWIDE TECHNOLOGY PROGRAMS MEET THE NEEDS OF DIVERSE LEARNERS

The administrator created twenty-five potential solutions to the problem of using technology meeting the diverse needs of learners.

Administrator's One Hundred Ideas

Provide training for teachers and administrators to understand and respect diverse cultural backgrounds, ensuring technology use is culturally sensitive.	Integrate multilingual interfaces and support in educational software and devices to assist students who speak languages other than the primary language of instruction.	Implement UDL principles in technology programs, offering multiple means of representation, engagement, and expression to cater to diverse learning styles.	Develop personalized technology-based learning plans for students with diverse needs, addressing their specific challenges and strengths.	Invest in technology devices that are accessible to students with disabilities, such as adaptive keyboards, screen readers, and other assistive technologies.
Offer ongoing professional development for teachers to enhance their skills in using adaptive technologies and accommodating diverse learners.	Collaborate with special education professionals to develop strategies and tools that address the unique requirements of students with disabilities.	Involve parents and community members in the decision-making process to understand the specific needs of diverse learners outside of the school environment.	Conduct regular assessments to identify the changing needs of diverse learners and adjust technology programs accordingly.	Design classrooms and learning spaces that can be easily adapted to accommodate various learning styles and physical abilities.
Establish peer mentoring programs where advanced students assist those who struggle, leveraging technology for collaborative learning.	Organize workshops for parents to familiarize them with the technology being used in schools, enabling better support for their children at home.	Encourage teachers to create inclusive digital content that represents diverse cultures, backgrounds, and perspectives.	Create channels for students to provide feedback on the effectiveness and accessibility of technology tools, fostering a sense of ownership and inclusion.	Implement learning management systems that are accessible to students with disabilities, ensuring they can fully participate in online learning activities.
Facilitate peer learning through collaborative online projects, allowing students to learn from each other and celebrate diversity.	Establish a tech support hotline where students and parents can seek assistance with technology-related issues, ensuring everyone can effectively use the tools provided.	Involve diverse voices in the development of the curriculum, ensuring it is culturally responsive and relatable to all students.	Continuously review school policies related to technology use to identify and eliminate any barriers or biases that might affect diverse learners.	Develop assessment that accommodates diverse learning styles, allowing students to demonstrate their understanding through various formats, including multimedia presentations and oral exams.
Collaborate with educational technology companies to develop customized solutions that cater to the specific needs of diverse learners.	Implement peer evaluation methods where students provide feedback to each other, promoting empathy, understanding, and acceptance among diverse groups.	Offer digital literacy programs that teach students how to critically evaluate online information, promoting awareness and understanding of diverse perspectives.	Allocate budgets flexibly, ensuring that funds are available for purchasing a variety of technology tools and software that cater to diverse needs.	Use data analytics to track the performance of diverse learners and adjust technology programs based on their individual progress and challenges.

The administrator then considered their capacity for two specific solutions. As you can see, the administrator has different amounts of capacity depending on the selected solution. For example, they have some support for redesigning the physical layout of classrooms but no support for implementing different models of learning. The administrator then completed the influence circles.

Administrator's Capacity Considerations

Capacity Considerations	
Design classrooms and learning spaces that can be easily adapted to accommodate various learning styles and physical abilities.	Implement UDL principles in technology programs, offering multiple means of representation, engagement, and expression to cater to diverse learning styles.

Level of Capacity						
LOTS OF CAPACITY	People	Mental Space			Time	Physical Space
SOME CAPACITY	Time	Physical Space	Support	Funds	Mental Space	People
NO CAPACITY	Supplies	Funds	Policy	Support	Policy	Supplies

Administrator's Level of Influence

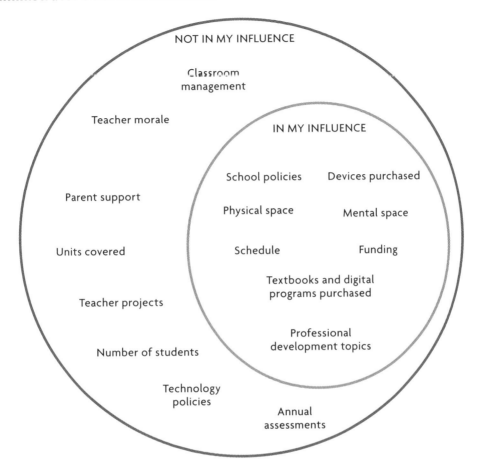

 ISTE Standards: For Education Leaders

3.4b: Ensure that resources for supporting the effective use of technology for learning are sufficient and scalable to meet future demand (ISTE, 2018).

3.5d: Develop the skills needed to lead and navigate change, advance systems and promote a mindset of continuous improvement for how technology can improve learning (ISTE, 2018).

WHAT HAPPENS NEXT?

Now that you have created potential solutions, considered your capacity, and explored your current levels of influence, it's time to decide which solution is the most appropriate to solve your problem. The next several chapters will explore the categories of the *Putting Out Fires* Framework in detail to help you select the best solution. Grab the extinguisher. It's time to put out the fire!

CHAPTER 5
EXTINGUISH THE EMBERS

WHEN A PROBLEM IS URGENT, we often implement the quick and easy solution—and wind up in an endless cycle of response. The quick and easy solution may be simple for now, but soon the problem will reoccur, leading to frustration. Implementing an immediate but incomplete solution can buy you time, but be aware that it can sometimes cause more problems than the one already in existence. The Extinguish category requires the least amount of capacity and addresses the problem quickly, but it generally does not solve the problem entirely, so the problem will likely reoccur. The *Putting Out Fires* Framework is not a leveling system. Solutions in the Extinguish category are not "right" or "wrong." The most effective solution to each problem you face will likely require differing capacities. Solutions in the Extinguish category are a great place to start when you need immediate relief from the problem. In future chapters, we will look at the other categories for longer-term solutions.

THE COOLING METHOD

Applying cool water is one of the most common methods used to extinguish actual fires. Cool water is used because its application "cools fuel to a point where it does not produce sufficient vapor to burn, with the reduction in temperature dependent on the application of an adequate flow of water to establish a negative heat balance" (National Fire Chiefs Council, n.d.). The cooling method specifically calls for water, not simply any liquid. Adding certain liquids (gasoline, for example) would cause the fire to grow rapidly.

We do the same thing with problems that arise in our schools. We view the problem and assume one solution will work yet when implementing that solution we are actually pouring gasoline onto a growing problem. Like the cooling method, what we really need to use is a specific liquid—water, thus, a specific solution. Implementing appropriate solutions to problems within the Extinguish category is akin to using cool water on a fire.

PROBLEMS BEST SOLVED WITH AN EXTINGUISH SOLUTION

Solutions in the Extinguish category work best to solve problems that require immediate action or smaller amounts of capacity and resources. Extinguish solutions do solve the problem in the moment, but without further action, the problem will likely reoccur. As an educator, you know that some problems must be solved *now*, and that a more effective solution may require more extensive resources.

A few years ago, I worked with a teacher with decades of experience who was very resistant to a request to begin using technology with her students. Her resistance had become a serious issue, because the school planned to launch a 1:1 program. In chatting with this teacher, I realized that she was simply afraid that her inexperience with technology would cause something terrible to happen, and she would not know what to do. I quickly implemented an Extinguish solution by co-teaching with this teacher to use technology in the classroom at every available opportunity. Today she is leading the digital charge in her secure school classroom. After attending specialized professional development, she not only champions blended learning in the classroom; she also asked to be part of new edtech initiatives. The simple solution of co-teaching with her quickly addressed her fear, while we moved quickly to offer practical professional development workshops with her in mind.

SOLUTIONS IN THE EXTINGUISH CATEGORY

A solution in the Extinguish category requires limited capacity and resources. These solutions should not be expensive, time consuming, or resource intensive. It is also important to note that the process of evaluating a solution is very personal and subjective. There is never a right or wrong answer—that is the beauty of design thinking. You can always make changes, prototype ideas, and pilot those ideas. With each step, you refine and clarify the solution. It can be challenging for educators to live in a space where there is no clear right or wrong. However, it can be helpful to shift your mindset from "Is this right or wrong?" to "Is this working or not working?" Also, one solution can solve a singular problem in one school but not another, in one classroom but not across the grade level, and for one student but not for all. As we explore the other categories of the *Putting Out Fires* Framework, other potential solutions will be more complex and require more capacity to pilot and implement—but might be a better fit for your specific problem in the long run. Solutions in the Extinguish category are best used when immediate relief from a problem is needed or when a solution involves low levels of capacity and resources.

INNOVATIVE EXTINGUISH SOLUTIONS

A great example of an innovative solution in the Extinguish category is found in the idea of a Friendship Bench. In an article published by the Association of American Medical Colleges, Stacy Weiner reported that in 2019, "One out of every five people in the United States had a mental illness" (2022). Toward the end of the pandemic, as of June, 2022, the number had grown to thirty-three percent. Access to resources to combat mental illness was a real problem that needed an immediate solution. The easiest solution was to ensure people suffering from mental illness had access to a local psychiatrist; however, there was (and still is) a massive shortage of psychiatrists. Weiner found that "the gap between need and access is wider among some populations, including those in rural areas. In fact, more than half of US counties lack a single psychiatrist" (2022).

In Zimbabwe, the situation was even more critical. Dr. Dixon Chibanda was "one of only fifteen psychiatrists in a country of sixteen million people" (Samuel, 2023). When Dr. Chibanda lost a patient because she could not afford the bus fare to see him, he knew this problem required an immediate solution. Chibanda realized that he had ample access to a group of people already scattered throughout the country who were seen as "experienced, empathetic, respected caregivers" (Samuel, 2023). Chibanda was referencing grandmothers! In his culture, grandmothers are widely respected.

He launched his solution immediately with fourteen grandmothers, training them in what he called "problem-solving therapy." The original group of grandmothers provided their services in "a simple, unpretentious, and accessible location: a park bench" (Samuel, 2023). The grandmothers (**Figure 5.1**) felt that meeting with the program participants on a park bench would eliminate the stigma and shame often associated with needing resources for mental health. Thus, the Friendship Bench program began as an immediate step towards providing free and easy access to mental health resources.

Many researchers have conducted studies on the Friendship Bench program. Munetsi et al. (2018), and Verhey et al. (2021), found that the program was in fact successful at lowering common mental disorder symptoms in participants meeting with the grandmothers. In 2022, The Friendship Bench program reached over 60,000 people in Zimbabwe (Samuel, 2023). In the last few years, the program has expanded to other countries including Kenya, Vietnam, and the US (Samuel, 2023).

FIGURE 5.1 Grandmother (right) with a client during a session at a Friendship Bench in Harare, Zimbabwe (Samuel, 2023).

The Friendship Bench program is a perfect example of those found in the Extinguish category because it quickly addressed the problem and involved very few resources to get started. The grandmothers were trained on problem-solving therapy in a matter of days and then began taking up their posts. Remember, Chibanda was one of the only psychiatrists in his country. In less than a week, he was able to essentially double the amount of people providing support to combat mental health issues. And, with the quick success of the program, the number of trained grandmothers kept growing until they were spread out all over the country.

This is such a great example of how an Extinguish solution can quickly solve a problem. A simple solution can be extremely innovative without requiring major resources.

FIRE DRILL!

Welcome to your next Fire Drill! You can now put into practice what you've learned throughout this chapter by looking at your list of solutions and finding those that fit into the Extinguish category. Scan the QR code to hear more detailed instructions from the author about the activities in this section.

kaylahholland.com/
puttingoutfires/audio

ADD SOLUTIONS TO THE EXTINGUISH CATEGORY

The Extinguish category includes solutions that can be implemented quickly to address the problem while likely not solving the problem entirely. Look at the list of solutions you created in the Fire Drill! section of Chapter 4 and find those that fit into the Extinguish category.

Extinguish

EXPLORE SOLUTIONS

From the Extinguish solutions listed above, select one specific solution. Answer the questions below to further explore the one specific solution selected (Lewrick et al., 2020, p. 72, 108).

POF	What is the level of immediacy for implementing this solution?	
WHO	Who does the solution impact?	
	Who are the decision makers?	
	Who are the allies?	
	Who are the obstacles?	
WHAT	What happens once the solution is implemented?	
	What other symptoms are affected?	
	What are the positive interactions?	
	What are the negative interactions?	
WHEN	When will you know the solution is successful?	
	When will you know if adjustments need to be made to the solution?	
HOW	How does the environment change when the solution is implemented?	
	How does the solution directly impact the problem (cause, symptom, etc.)?	

LIKE, WISH, WONDER

Using the selected solution from the previous activity, answer the three prompts in the activity below. What do you like about the solution (positive comments); what do you wish to see (positive criticisms); what do you wonder (questions) (Lewrick et al., 2020, p. 240).

LIKE

What do you like?
Positive comments

WISH

What do you wish?
Positive critiques

WONDER

What do you wonder?
Questions you have

SAMPLE PROBLEMS

Let's check in with our sample problems introduced in Chapter 2. How did the teacher and administrator complete the activities in the Fire Drill! section for this chapter?

TEACHER: PURPOSEFUL TECHNOLOGY USE TO ENHANCE STUDENT LEARNING

Looking at potential solutions that fit into the Extinguish category helps you see which options could be implemented immediately. The teacher has seven solutions in the Extinguish category and selects: "facilitate collaborative projects that require students to work together online, promoting teamwork and digital communication skills."

Teacher's Extinguish Solutions

Extinguish

Create online repositories of educational technology tools, lesson plans, and resources for teachers to access and implement in their classrooms.	Integrate educational games and gamified elements into the curriculum, making learning more engaging and interactive for students.	Foster creativity by encouraging students to create digital stories, videos, and presentations to demonstrate their understanding of various subjects.	Facilitate collaborate projects that require students to work together online, promoting teamwork and digital communication skills.
Leverage social media platforms to create educational communities, where students can discuss topics, share resources, and collaborate on projects.	Foster communities of practice where teachers can share their experiences, challenges, and successes related to technology integration.	Invest in research to continuously evaluate the impact of technology on student learning, adapting strategies based on evidence-based practices.	

The teacher explores further by answering several questions about the selected solution and listing what they like, wish, and wonder about the solution. For example, the teacher likes that the solution can be implemented quickly but wonders if it will last beyond one new activity and really solve the problem?

Teacher's Solution Exploration

POF	What is the level of immediacy for implementing this solution?	This solution can be implemented within two days.
WHO	Who does the solution impact?	Students and teachers
	Who are the decision makers?	Teachers and principals
	Who are the allies?	Students and teachers
	Who are the obstacles?	Students and teachers
WHAT	What happens once the solution is implemented?	Students create collaborative digital projects within their classes.
	What other symptoms are affected?	Lack of engagement in content
	What are the positive interactions?	Collaboration with peers
	What are the negative interactions?	Not tied to academics and seen as a standalone activity
WHEN	When will you know the solution is successful?	Students complete digital collaborative projects
	When will you know if adjustments need to be made to the solutions?	When teachers return to their normal routine without using tech to enhance learning
HOW	How does the environment change when the solution is implemented?	It only changes for a short time while projects are being completed
	How does the solution directly impact the problem (cause, symptom, etc.)?	The solution directly impacts the lack of student engagement by creating an interesting digital activity for students to complete.

Teacher's Like, Wish, Wonder Activity

LIKE

What do you like?
Positive comments

I like that this solution can be implemented quickly and encourages students to collaborate digitally with their peers.

WISH

What do you wish?
Positive critiques

I wish the solution created a larger and longer-lasting impact rather than just one project.

WONDER

What do you wonder?
Questions you have

I wonder if this solution will encourage teachers to implement this type of project on a more regular basis.

 ISTE Standards: For Educators

2.2a: Shape, advance and accelerate a shared vision for empowered learning with technology by engaging with education stakeholders (ISTE, 2017).

2.6c: Create learning opportunities that challenge students to use a design process and computational thinking to innovate and solve problems (ISTE, 2017).

ADMINISTRATOR: ENSURING SCHOOLWIDE TECHNOLOGY PROGRAMS MEET THE NEEDS OF DIVERSE LEARNERS

Looking at potential solutions that fit into the Extinguish category helps to see which options can be implemented immediately. The administrator has seven solutions in the Extinguish category and selects: "encourage teachers to create inclusive digital content that represents diverse cultures, backgrounds, and perspectives."

Administrator's Extinguish Solutions

Extinguish

Collaborate with special education professionals to develop strategies and tools that address the unique requirements of students with disabilities.	Establish peer mentoring programs where advanced students assist those who struggle, leveraging technology for collaborative learning.	Encourage teachers to create inclusive digital content that represents diverse cultures, backgrounds, and perspectives.	Involve diverse voices in the development of the curriculum, ensuring it is culturally responsive and relatable to all students.
Continuously review school policies related to technology use to identify and eliminate any barriers or biases that might affect diverse learners.	Allocate budgets flexibly, ensuring that funds are available for purchasing a variety of technology tools and software that cater to diverse needs.	Invest in research to continuously evaluate the impact of technology on student learning, adapting strategies based on evidence-based practices.	

The administrator explores further by answering several questions about the selected solution and listing what they like, wish, and wonder about the solution. For example, the administrator likes that this solution can be implemented quickly but wonders if it will create the type of culture change needed to solve the problem.

Administrator's Solution Exploration

POF	What is the level of immediacy for implementing this solution?	This solution can be implemented quickly once training has been offered to clarify what inclusive content means and what is appropriate.
WHO	Who does the solution impact?	Students and teachers
	Who are the decision makers?	Teachers and principals
	Who are the allies?	Students and teachers
	Who are the obstacles?	Teachers and principals
WHAT	What happens once the solution is implemented?	Teachers begin using culturally appropriate content and materials representing diverse cultures in the classroom.
	What other symptoms are affected?	Lack of engagement in content, students feeling out of place.
	What are the positive interactions?	Students feeling included
	What are the negative interactions?	Not tied to academic content and seen as a standalone activity or an inauthentic required task
WHEN	When will you know the solution is successful?	When diverse content is being authentically selected and implemented in classrooms.
	When will you know if adjustments need to be made to the solution?	When teachers return to their normal content without thinking about the diverse needs of their students.
HOW	How does the environment change when the solution is implemented?	It only changes for a short time while the initiative is being pushed by the administration.
	How does the solution directly impact the problem (cause, symptom, etc.)?	The solution directly impacts the lack of diversity in digital content.

Administrator's Like, Wish, Wonder Activity

LIKE

What do you like?
Positive comments

I like that this solution can be implemented quickly and that it encourages teachers to consider the content taught in their classrooms.

WISH

What do you wish?
Positive critiques

I wish the solution created a larger and longer-lasting impact rather than simply encouraging teachers to create inclusive content.

WONDER

What do you wonder?
Questions you have

I wonder if this solution will encourage teachers to change their content for the entire year or just while the initiative is being pushed by the administration.

 ISTE Standards: For Education Leaders

3.2b: Engage education stakeholders in developing and adopting a shared vision for using technology to improve student success, informed by the learning sciences (ISTE, 2018).

3.5c: Use technology to regularly engage in reflective practices that support personal and professional growth (ISTE, 2018).

WHAT HAPPENS NEXT?

Now that you have explored solutions in the Extinguish category and understand that these solutions quickly assess and address the problem with a simple solution, let's explore how to smother the fire using the Detect category in the next chapter.

CHAPTER 6
DETECT
THE FLAMES

SOLUTIONS IN THE DETECT CATEGORY allow us to understand all facets of a problem, gather input from the people the problem impacts, and understand the symptoms of the problem. Unlike the Extinguish category, solutions in the Detect category are not implemented immediately; instead, these types of solutions require time and effort, and offer an entirely new perspective. A Detect solution keeps the problem at bay for a longer period of time than solutions in the Extinguish category. Solutions in the Detect category ask us to study the problem at hand from multiple perspectives to determine which solution is the most practical.

THE SMOTHERING METHOD

One way to put out real fires is to use a method known as smothering. The smothering process prevents "fresh air from reaching the seat of the fire, allowing the combustion to reduce the oxygen content in the confined atmosphere until it extinguishes itself" (National Fire Chiefs Council, n.d.). Similar to snuffing out a candle, the idea of smothering is to cover the fire, thus removing the fire's access to fresh air and causing it to self-extinguish.

The smothering technique also works with solutions in the Detect category. When we implement a solution within the Detect category, we analyze the problem and design a solution directed specifically at the symptoms of the problem itself. By targeting the symptoms of the problem, the solution is more likely to be successful and last longer than solutions in the Extinguish category. Solutions in this category can be found by using a design-thinking approach to understand the root causes of the problem and understand specific symptoms with any solutions designed.

PROBLEMS BEST SOLVED WITH A DETECT SOLUTION

The types of problems that lend themselves best to solutions in the Detect category are those that require research, data collection, observation, focus groups, surveys, and other methods of collecting information. These types of problems usually have a larger and longer-lasting impact on the school than problems in the Extinguish category. These types of problems will not go away and will likely become worse without the right solution in place. It may be difficult to take the time needed to evaluate, process data, and effectively address this problem, but in the end, it will be worthwhile.

A couple of years ago, students over the age of eighteen were allowed to opt out of educational programming in one secure school. The administrators began to track the opt-out students to determine the reasons behind their decision. Administrators realized students were opting out for one of three reasons, including that the programs being offered were uninteresting and would not help them become more successful after being released. More data was obtained about what types of programs students were interested in, and with those results, administrators began offering additional classes in trade skills such as culinary arts, construction, haircutting, and more. Using a Detect solution took time to collect data and analyze the results but the eventual solution implemented was highly impactful for the students in this secure school as they were given access to trade skills that will help them obtain stable jobs.

SOLUTIONS IN THE DETECT CATEGORY

A solution in the Detect category will include new ways to address the problem after analyzing the symptoms and root causes of the problem itself. The timeline for piloting may be longer, and your success will likely require the participation of multiple stakeholders. Strong communication is key, and you must be willing to hit the pause button to gather more information to design a prototype that will become a successful pilot leading to a fully implemented solution.

AN INNOVATIVE DETECT SOLUTION

An innovative example of a Detect solution began in Edward Palmer's 1973 study on television for children. Palmer's study addressed the "systemic use of broadcast television to promote the social, emotional, and intellectual growth of young children" (1973). Palmer found that young children were exposed to "upwards of thirty hours of television fare each week" and that not enough research had been conducted to plan appropriate content to address proper learning development (1973).

At the time, *Sesame Street* was a popular children's television show. Palmer found a lack of research and communication between the show's production company and educational research teams, and asserted that *Sesame Street* could not be viewed as a successful example of educational television.

In the book *The Tipping Point*, Malcolm Gladwell discusses Palmer's research in this area. Gladwell details how Palmer changed educational television by determining that presenting ideas in an engaging way makes learning more memorable, because viewers are actively involved and not simply a passive audience (Gladwell, 2002). Gladwell's example of successful educational children's programming is *Blue's Clues*. The creators of Blue's Clues made the show length half an hour instead of a whole hour and constructed every episode in the exact same way, while also offering children a chance to participate actively.

The educational information presented by the two shows is extremely similar: both aim to help young children understand basic concepts before starting preschool. The differences are found in how the information is presented. *Sesame Street* is consumed more passively while *Blue's Clues*'s viewers participate actively (Gladwell, 2002). Gladwell notes that "within months of its debut in 1996, *Blue's Clues* was trouncing *Sesame Street* in the ratings" (Gladwell, 2002). Blue's Clues is an innovative response to the problem of passive consumption of educational children's programming.

When viewing this problem within our Detect category, we can easily see the problem and successful solution. The problem was that educational television in the late '60s did not exist, and *Sesame Street* worked to fill that void. What we learned from Palmer is that not enough research was completed to truly understand the problem itself or the intended audience. After further research was conducted, one of the symptoms of the lack of impact was found to be that Sesame Street was not truly solving the problem because of the attempt to entertain both adults and children. When the creators of Blue's Clues narrowed their focus because they knew the exact symptom, they were able to create a successful solution.

Problems in the Detect category need to be studied and analyzed. When we understand the true symptoms of the problem itself, we can create a successful solution. However, creating a solution that only somewhat solves the intended problem (e.g., designing content for adults and children) lowers the overall impact of the solution itself and will most likely result in the problem returning in the future. Understanding the true symptoms of the problem is essential to implementing the best solution for the longest possible impact.

 FIRE DRILL!

Welcome to your next Fire Drill! You can now put into practice what you've learned throughout this chapter by looking at your list of solutions and finding those that fit into the Detect category. Scan the QR code to hear more detailed instructions from the author about the activities in this section.

**kaylahholland.com/
puttingoutfires/audio**

ADD SOLUTIONS TO THE DETECT CATEGORY

The Detect category includes solutions that require further study of the problem and directly impact symptoms of the problem. Look at the list of solutions you created in the Fire Drill! section of Chapter 4, and list any potential solutions that fit into the Detect category using the space below.

Detect

EXPLORE SOLUTIONS

From the Detect solutions you listed in the activity above, select one specific solution. Using the table below, answer the questions to further explore the solution you selected (Lewrick et al., 2020, p. 72, 108).

POF	List at least two specific symptoms from the problem.	
WHO	Who does the solution impact?	
	Who are the decision makers?	
	Who are the allies?	
	Who are the obstacles?	
WHAT	What happens once the solution is implemented?	
	What other symptoms are affected?	
	What are the positive interactions?	
	What are the negative interactions?	
WHEN	When will you know the solution is successful?	
	When will you know if adjustments need to be made to the solution?	
HOW	How does the environment change when the solution is implemented?	
	How does the solution directly impact the problem (cause, symptom, etc.)?	

LIKE, WISH, WONDER

Using the selected solution from the previous activity, answer the three prompts in the spaces below.

1. What do you like about the solution (positive comments)?
2. What do you wish to see from implementing this solution (positive criticisms)?
3. What do you wonder (questions)? (Lewrick et al., 2020, p. 240).

LIKE

What do you like?
Positive comments

WISH

What do you wish?
Positive critiques

WONDER

What do you wonder?
Questions you have

SAMPLE PROBLEMS

Let's check in with our sample problems, introduced in Chapter 1. How did the teacher and administrator complete the activities in the Fire Drill! section for this chapter?

TEACHER: PURPOSEFUL TECHNOLOGY USE TO ENHANCE STUDENT LEARNING

Looking at potential solutions that fit into the Detect category helps to see options to address all the symptoms involved by collecting data and studying the problem from multiple angles. The teacher has five solutions in the Detect category and selects: "use data analytics to track students' progress and identify areas where technology integration has been particularly effective or needs improvement."

Teacher's Detect Solutions

Detect

Encourage the flipped classroom approach, where students engage with digital content at home and utilize classroom time for discussions and collaborative activities.	Organize podcasts and webinars with industry experts, giving students access to real-world insights and experiences.	Use data analytics to track students' progress and identify areas where technology integration has been particularly effective or needs improvement.	Ensure that all devices and software used in classrooms are up to date, providing a seamless user experience for both teachers and students.
Conduct regular workshops and training sessions to educate teachers about effective and purposeful use of technology in the classroom.			

The teacher explores the solution by answering several questions and listing what they like, wish, and wonder about the solution. For example, the teacher likes that this solution collects data but wonders if the data will show student engagement, or simply how technology is currently being used?

Teacher's Solution Exploration

POF	List at least two specific symptoms from the problem.	Bored students, lack of interest, tech becomes a substitute for paper
WHO	Who does the solution impact?	Students and teachers
	Who are the decision makers?	Principals
	Who are the allies?	Principals
	Who are the obstacles?	Superintendent or finance
WHAT	What happens once the solution is implemented?	Data tracks student use of technology to determine gaps
	What other symptoms are affected?	Lack of engagement in content, gaps in digital resources
	What are the positive interactions?	Data shows where technology is helping to fill current gaps
	What are the negative interactions?	Data shows more gaps than were known before
WHEN	When will you know the solution is successful?	When there is enough data to make knowledgeable decisions about tech programs
	When will you know if adjustments need to be made to the solutions?	When the data collected isn't clear enough to make decisions
HOW	How does the environment change when the solution is implemented?	Other technology can be purchased and implemented to fill gaps found
	How does the solution directly impact the problem (cause, symptom, etc.)?	The solution directly impacts the lack of student engagement by using data to track how technology is used currently to make informed decisions.

Teacher's Like, Wish, Wonder Activity

LIKE

What do you like?
Positive comments

I like that this solution can be implemented quickly and encourages students to collaborate digitally with their peers.

WISH

What do you wish?
Positive critiques

I wish the solution created a larger and longer-lasting impact rather than just one project.

WONDER

What do you wonder?
Questions you have

I wonder if this solution will encourage teachers to implement this type of project on a more regular basis.

 ### ISTE Standards: For Educators

2.2a: Shape, advance and accelerate a shared vision for empowered learning with technology by engaging with education stakeholders (ISTE, 2017).

2.6c: Create learning opportunities that challenge students to use a design process and computational thinking to innovate and solve problems (ISTE, 2017).

ADMINISTRATOR: ENSURING SCHOOLWIDE TECHNOLOGY PROGRAMS MEET THE NEEDS OF DIVERSE LEARNERS

Looking at potential solutions that fit into the Detect category helps to see options to address all the symptoms involved by collecting data and studying the problem from multiple angles. The administrator has five solutions in the Detect category and selects: "use data analytics to track the performance of diverse learners and adjust technology programs based on their individual progress and challenges."

Administrator's Detect Solutions

Detect

Offer ongoing professional development for teachers to enhance their skills in using adaptive technologies and accommodating diverse learners.

Conduct regular assessments to identify the changing needs of diverse learners and adjust technology problems accordingly.

Create channels for students to provide feedback on the effectiveness and accessibility of technology tools, fostering a sense of ownership and inclusion.

Develop assessments that accommodate diverse learning styles, allowing students to demonstrate their understanding through various formats, including multimedia presentations and oral exams.

Use data analytics to track the performance of diverse learners and adjust technology programs based on their individual progress and challenges.

The administrator explores the solution by answering several questions and lists what they like, wish, and wonder about the solution. For example, the administrator likes that the solution will collect data but wishes it would also track how the student feels about technology meeting their needs.

Administrator's Solution Exploration

POF	List at least two specific symptoms from the problem.	Tech not meeting diverse learner needs, students feeling out of place
WHO	Who does the solution impact?	Students
	Who are the decision makers?	Principals
	Who are the allies?	Principals
	Who are the obstacles?	Superintendent or finance
WHAT	What happens once the solution is implemented?	Data tracks use of technology to determine gaps in meeting the needs of all students
	What other symptoms are affected?	Lack of engagement in content, gaps in digital resources available
	What are the positive interactions?	Data shows where technology is helping to meet the needs of diverse learners
	What are the negative interactions?	Data shows more needs than were known before
WHEN	When will you know the solution is successful?	When there is enough data to make knowledgeable decisions about tech programs moving forward
	When will you know if adjustments need to be made to the solutions?	When the data collected isn't clear enough to make decisions
HOW	How does the environment change when the solution is implemented?	Current technology can be used to meet the diverse needs of students OR more technology can be purchased
	How does the solution directly impact the problem (cause, symptom, etc.)?	The solution directly impacts the diverse needs of learners because the tracked data is used to make informed decisions

Administrator's Like, Wish, Wonder Activity

LIKE

What do you like?
Positive comments

I like that this solution can be implemented quickly and that it allows the collected data to determine if the current needs of diverse learners are being met or if more technology is needed.

WISH

What do you wish?
Positive critiques

I wish the solution could also track how students feel about the current technology meeting their needs.

WONDER

What do you wonder?
Questions you have

I wonder if this solution will actually impact the problem or if it will only show how digital programs are currently being used to meet the diverse needs of learners, and if that will be shown as a positive or a negative.

 ISTE Standards: For Education Leaders

3.2b: Engage education stakeholders in developing and adopting a shared vision for using technology to improve student success, informed by the learning sciences (ISTE, 2018).

3.5c: Use technology to regularly engage in reflective practices that support personal and professional growth (ISTE, 2018).

WHAT HAPPENS NEXT?

Now that you understand solutions in the Detect category, continue to the next chapter to learn how to starve the fire with solutions from the Contain category.

CHAPTER 7
CONTAIN THE BLAZE

WHEN A SOLUTION FALLS INTO THE CONTAIN CATEGORY, the problem itself is confined to study one or more causes of the problem. Problems that require containment are often harmful to people or involve a solution that cannot be implemented without first understanding all potential causes of the problem itself. Some people simply contain the problem and move on without implementing a true solution because they have relief from the problem at the time. If the problem is contained without an appropriate solution implemented, no changes will be made to the problem itself and the problem will return. The main goal of solutions in the Contain category is to quickly contain the problem to study the underlying causes of the problem itself before designing and implementing a practical solution.

THE STARVATION METHOD

One method of putting out real fires is called starvation. In the starvation method, you literally remove items that fuel the fire from the path of the fire itself to starve the fire from the source it needs to grow. For example, removing items such as vehicles, tires, cargo, or anything containing fuel from the path of the fire will cause the fire itself to consume all its own fuel and extinguish itself (National Fire Chiefs Council, n.d.). The same idea is true for problems in the Contain category. Once you contain the problem itself, you can study the causes of the problem and implement a solution to address the causes directly.

PROBLEMS BEST SOLVED WITH A CONTAIN SOLUTION

The types of problems that lend themselves best to solutions in the Contain category are those where a solution cannot be implemented without first understanding the causes of the problem itself. These types of problems will not go away on their own and are likely to cause harm to others. Also, without an appropriate solution in place, this problem will continue to become worse. Implementing a solution that applies directly to the causes themselves leads to real and lasting change with minimal negative impact.

A consistent problem in secure schools is a high turnover of teachers, often leaving principals with vacancies lasting an entire school year. One principal opted to implement virtual instruction instead of filling the vacancies with onsite teachers. The same funding available for teacher salaries was rerouted to fund the virtual program. The principal thought virtual instruction would be better than no instruction at all because while using the virtual program is not ideal, it does help to contain the issue. Using a Contain solution was an excellent choice in this instance because it allowed the principal to contain the problem using virtual instruction while continuing to recruit on-site teachers for the following year.

SOLUTIONS IN THE CONTAIN CATEGORY

Solutions in the Contain category address a problem that cannot be solved without first containing the problem and studying the causes directly. The solution will include innovative ways to address the problem after analyzing all causes involved. The solution might require major changes to the typical structure of the school day (e.g., policies, procedures, professional development, or schedules) but it is vital to address all causes and to have open communication with the people involved to fully implement the best possible solution.

Implementing a solution without fully understanding all causes will eventually lead to more harm being done to those experiencing the problem. Therefore, it is crucial for solutions in this category to not only contain the problem but to understand all potential causes so a more beneficial solution can be implemented.

AN INNOVATIVE CONTAIN SOLUTION

An innovative example of a solution in the Contain category can be found in Australia. In 2022, the number of deaths on rural roads increased by 30% over the previous year, with almost half caused by vehicles running off the road (Schapova, 2022). Civil engineers at Tarmac Linemarking thought of a creative solution—to illuminate lines on the road with glow-in-the-dark strips (Evans, 2022). Tarmac Linemarkings began a trial in May, 2022, by marking a half mile using photoluminescent line markings along with seventy other locations as part of the Department of Transport's $457 million Victorian Government Road Safety Program (Schapova, 2022). This innovative solution was successful because the strips, using a similar process to glow-in-the-dark stickers and toys, absorb sun during the day so that at night they emit a light that's easily seen by drivers (**Figure 7.1**). The goal of the photoluminescent strips is to provide drivers with a "stronger visual signal to follow in low light" (Evans, 2022). This solution effectively solves the problem of road deaths due to vehicles running off the road in rural areas because it essentially lights the path so the road is clear for drivers (Schapova, 2022).

FIGURE 7.1

A road in Australia marked with photoluminescent strips. (Evans, 2022)

When viewing this problem within our Contain category, we can easily see the problem and successful solution. The problem was that the percentage of vehicle accidents in rural areas had increased drastically due to vehicles running off the road. The problem was contained with a quick innovative solution to place photoluminescent strips along seventy sections of rural highways. The problem was contained while further studies were being conducted to ensure this was the best solution for the problem and that the solution implemented was both effective and efficient before implementing the solution on a larger scale. The solution is effective because the prominent cause of the issue was identified. A direct solution was created because the identified problem was that drivers were running vehicles off the road at night and in rural areas. Without knowing the actual cause of this problem, a successful solution would have been difficult to implement.

Problems in the Contain category need to be contained and then studied to determine the true cause of the problem. When we understand the cause of the problem itself, we can create a successful solution. However, containing the problem and implementing a solution without taking the time to fully understand the cause lowers the overall impact of the solution itself and will likely result in the problem returning.

 # FIRE DRILL!

Welcome to your next Fire Drill! You can now put into practice what you've learned throughout this chapter by looking at your list of solutions and finding those that fit into the Contain category. Scan the QR code to hear more detailed instructions from the author about the activities in this section.

kaylahholland.com/
puttingoutfires/audio

ADD SOLUTIONS TO THE CONTAIN CATEGORY

The Contain category includes solutions that quickly contain the problem so that it can be further studied and cause minimal impact. Look at the list of solutions created in the Fire Drill! section of Chapter 4, and list any potential solutions that fit into the Contain category using the activity below.

Contain

EXPLORE SOLUTIONS

Using the Contain solutions listed in the activity above, select one specific solution. In the activity below, answer the questions to further explore that solution (Lewrick et al., 2020, p. 72, 108).

POF	List at least two direct causes of the problem.	
WHO	Who does the solution impact?	
	Who are the decision makers?	
	Who are the allies?	
	Who are the obstacles?	
WHAT	What happens once the solution is implemented?	
	What other symptoms are affected?	
	What are the positive interactions?	
	What are the negative interactions?	
WHEN	When will you know the solution is successful?	
	When will you know if adjustments need to be made to the solutions?	
HOW	How does the environment change when the solution is implemented?	
	How does the solution directly impact the problem (cause, symptom, etc.)?	

LIKE, WISH, WONDER

Using the selected solution from the previous activity, answer the three prompts in the activity below. What do you like about the solution (positive comments); what do you wish to see (positive criticisms); what do you wonder (questions) (Lewrick et al., 2020, p. 240).

LIKE

What do you like?
Positive comments

WISH

What do you wish?
Positive critiques

WONDER

What do you wonder?
Questions you have

SAMPLE PROBLEMS

Let's check in with our sample problems introduced in Chapter 1. How did the teacher and administrator complete the activities in the Fire Drill! section for this chapter?

TEACHER: PURPOSEFUL TECHNOLOGY USE TO ENHANCE STUDENT LEARNING

Looking at potential solutions that fit into the Contain category helps to see which solutions directly address what is causing the problem. The teacher has six solutions in the Contain category and selects: "provide access to online tutorials and instructional videos that support classroom learning and cater to different learning styles."

Teacher's Contain Solutions

Contain

Encourage experienced teachers to mentor their peers, sharing successful strategies for integrating technology effectively.	Introduce digital assessment tools that provide instant feedback to both students and teachers, facilitating a more responsive learning environment.	Use cloud-based tools for document collaboration, allowing students and teachers to access and work on assignments from any device with an internet connection.	Provide access to online tutorials and instructional videos that support classroom learning and cater to different learning styles.
Integrate lessons on digital ethics, online safety, and responsible internet use to promote good digital citizenship among students.	Implement interactive online platforms that allow students to engage with educational content in a dynamic and personalized manner.		

The teacher explores the solution by answering several questions and listing what they like, wish, and wonder about the solution. For example, the teacher likes that this solution addresses their concerns about technology by providing more professional development, but the teacher wishes the solution did not depend on their ability to use and access technology

Teacher's Solution Exploration

POF	List at least two direct causes of the problem.	Lack of student interest, teacher's fear of using tech, lack of classroom management
WHO	Who does the solution impact?	Students and teachers
	Who are the decision makers?	Principals
	Who are the allies?	Teachers
	Who are the obstacles?	Students and principals
WHAT	What happens once the solution is implemented?	Teachers can access online tutorials on how to implement technology
	What other symptoms are affected?	Teacher fear of using technology
	What are the positive interactions?	Teacher gains knowledge about technology use
	What are the negative interactions?	Teacher has to use technology to learn more about technology—low tech skills could hinder learning
WHEN	When will you know the solution is successful?	When teachers are implementing technology successfully and regularly in their classrooms.
	When will you know if adjustments need to be made to the solutions?	When teachers return to their normal routine without using tech to enhance learning on a regular basis.
HOW	How does the environment change when the solution is implemented?	Classroom content becomes more relevant to students and technology is implemented purposefully into the classroom.
	How does the solution directly impact the problem (cause, symptom, etc.)?	The solution directly impacts the lack of student engagement by helping teachers become more knowledgeable about how to implement tech well.

Teacher's Like, Wish, Wonder Activity

LIKE

What do you like?
Positive comments

I like that this solution helps address the teacher concerns about using technology in the classroom by providing more instruction.

WISH

What do you wish?
Positive critiques

I wish the solution did not depend on teacher's ability with and access to technology.

WONDER

What do you wonder?
Questions you have

I wonder if this solution will be successful because if a teacher has a lower level of skill with technology, using technology to provide the training could be a huge barrier.

 ISTE Standards: For Educators

2.2a: Shape, advance and accelerate a shared vision for empowered learning with technology by engaging with education stakeholders (ISTE, 2017).

2.6c: Create learning opportunities that challenge students to use a design process and computational thinking to innovate and solve problems (ISTE, 2017).

ADMINISTRATOR: ENSURING SCHOOLWIDE TECHNOLOGY PROGRAMS MEET THE NEEDS OF DIVERSE LEARNERS

Looking at potential solutions that fit into the Contain category helps to see which solutions directly address what is causing the problem. The administrator has seven solutions in the Contain category and selects: "provide training for teachers and administrators to understand and respect diverse cultural backgrounds, ensuring technology use is culturally sensitive."

Administrator's Contain Solutions

Contain

Provide training for teachers and administrators to understand and respect diverse cultural backgrounds, ensuring technology use is culturally sensitive.

Develop personalized, technology-based learning plans for students with diverse needs, addressing their specific challenges and strengths.

Involve parents and community members in the decision-making process to understand the specific needs of diverse learners outside of the school environment.

Organize workshops for parents to familiarize them with the technology being used in schools, enabling better support for their children at home.

Encourage teachers to create inclusive digital content that represents diverse cultures, backgrounds, and perspectives.

Establish a tech support hotline where students and parents can seek assistance with technology-related issues, ensuring everyone can effectively use the tools provided.

Offer digital literacy programs that teach students how to critically evaluate online information, promoting awareness and understanding of diverse perspectives.

The administrator explores the solution by answering several questions and listing what they like, wish, and wonder about the solution. For example, the administrator likes that this solution addresses the problem at the teacher level but wonders if this solution will create authentic change or simply be a checklist item.

Administrator's Solution Exploration

POF	List at least three direct causes of the problem.	Teacher fear, students feeling isolated, low academic performance
WHO	Who does the solution impact?	Students and teachers
	Who are the decision makers?	Principals
	Who are the allies?	Teachers and students
	Who are the obstacles?	Teachers and principals
WHAT	What happens once the solution is implemented?	Teachers begin using culturally respectful digital content.
	What other symptoms are affected?	Students begin to feel like they belong.
	What are the positive interactions?	Teacher gains knowledge and students openly accept their culture and/or needs.
	What are the negative interactions?	Students feel this is done with authenticity.
WHEN	When will you know the solution is successful?	When teachers are implementing content that represents diverse cultures, perspectives, needs, and abilities.
	When will you know if adjustments need to be made to the solutions?	When teachers return to their normal content without considering the diverse needs of their learners.
HOW	How does the environment change when the solution is implemented?	Classrooms become a welcoming space for all students.
	How does the solution directly impact the problem (cause, symptom, etc.)?	The solution directly impacts the diverse needs of learners by providing teachers with training and creating a shared language and set of expectations.

Administrator's Like, Wish, Wonder Activity

LIKE

What do you like?
Positive comments

I like that this solution addresses the problem at the teacher level.

WISH

What do you wish?
Positive critiques

I wish the solution created a larger and longer-lasting impact rather than just one training session. We all need to learn about the diverse needs of learners, and one workshop will not effectively provide the content needed.

WONDER

What do you wonder?
Questions you have

I wonder if this solution will encourage teachers to change their content and teaching style to meet the diverse needs of their learners or if this will be a checklist item to complete.

 ## ISTE Standards: For Education Leaders

3.2b: Engage education stakeholders in developing and adopting a shared vision for using technology to improve student success, informed by the learning sciences (ISTE, 2018).

3.5c: Use technology to regularly engage in reflective practices that support personal and professional growth (ISTE, 2018).

WHAT HAPPENS NEXT?

Now that you have explored solutions that minimize the problem to a small space for further study, continue to the next chapter to explore ways to prevent the firestorm.

CHAPTER 8
PREVENT
THE FIRESTORM

SOLUTIONS IN THE PREVENT CATEGORY require the most time, resources, and capacity of the four categories, but completely solve the problem without fear of the problem returning. However, solutions in the Prevent category are not always the best option. The four categories in the *Putting Out Fires* Framework are not a leveling system. You can combine solutions in one or more categories, but you do not have to begin in the Extinguish category and work your way through to the Prevent category. The ideal category is selected when the focus of the problem is clear. For example, when we discussed solving the problem of children drowning in Chapter 2, the solution in the Prevent category was to completely drain the river of water. Draining the river solves the problem but does not stop children from drowning in another body of water. Also, draining the river may cause more problems than it solves. This is why the *Putting Out Fires* Framework is helpful because it allows us to categorize all potential solutions to select the most appropriate solution for the specific problem at hand.

THE INTERRUPTING METHOD

One method of putting out real fires is called the interrupting method. The interrupting method uses certain extinguishing agents to literally interrupt the chemical reaction taking place causing the fire (National Fire Chiefs Council, n.d.). A fire begins when fuel meets heat that creates an ignition causing a fire. The interrupting method uses an agent to interrupt the chemical process. For example, agents that interrupt the fire process are dry chemicals, foam, freezing water, and gaseous fire suppression (Voelkert, 2015). Before deploying an extinguishing agent, the impact of the method must first be considered. For example, will using the selected agent cause damage to people, the environment, or property (National Fire Chiefs Council, n.d.)?

This same idea is present when selecting solutions in the Prevent category. Before implementing a solution you must consider how the solution will impact the people and culture involved. When the symptoms and causes of problems are truly understood, a solution can be implemented that, like the interrupting method, will extinguish the problem without negatively affecting the people or area around the problem.

PROBLEMS BEST SOLVED WITH A PREVENT SOLUTION

The types of problems that lend themselves best to solutions in the Prevent category are those where a solution cannot be implemented without involving large amounts of time, resources, and people. These types of problems will not go away on their own and without an appropriate solution in place, will likely become worse.

A significant problem in secure schools is that only certain materials are allowed. With limited materials, science teachers are not able to implement many common science experiments, leaving students unable to engage with the science concepts taught. One solution to this problem is virtual reality (VR). VR headsets allow students to complete scientific experiments in classrooms without needing access to materials such as beakers, dissection tools, and more. Implementing the Prevent solution of VR into secure schools required lots of time, resources, and people, because we needed to research appropriate VR programs and test run several options in secure schools before feeling confident about one particular program. This process took almost eighteen months—from the first idea to the first VR implementation in a secure school. We were well-satisfied with our investment of time and effort when students in secure schools were able to successfully conduct science experiments, and additionally travel the world and gain exposure to a wide array of content they would not otherwise have been able to access.

SOLUTIONS IN THE PREVENT CATEGORY

A solution in the Prevent category requires capacity, influence, and resources. These solutions can be expensive and time consuming. It is also important to note that the amount of time you will spend evaluating and implementing a solution in the Prevent category is not trivial. You might design a solution, implement a pilot, gather feedback, and make changes to the solution before implementing it on a larger scale. With each step, you refine and clarify the solution. You should also include a variety of voices in the solution design process to ensure that what is implemented will have a positive impact on all stakeholders. Other categories of the *Putting Out Fires* Framework are less complex and require less capacity to implement, but might be a better fit for certain problems. Solutions in the Prevent category require ample access to resources and the influence to make changes in affected areas.

AN INNOVATIVE PREVENT SOLUTION

Finland has been attempting to reduce homelessness in its country since the early 80s. They started by building short-term shelters. This solution is the most common across the globe for addressing homelessness. Typically, "those affected are expected to look for a job and free themselves from their psychological problems or addictions. Only then do they get help in finding accommodation" (Glösel, 2023). This solution was less than successful, and in 2008 the Finnish government adopted a new solution called Housing First to reduce the number of homeless people. Housing First reverses the former process of requiring the homeless to end addiction or psychological problems before receiving lodging. Housing First believes that people are more likely to move forward successfully if they receive housing first (Hancock, 2022). Once they receive housing, "social workers help them with applications for social benefits and are available for counseling in general. In such a new, secure situation, it is easier for those affected to find a job and take care of their physical and mental health" (Glösel, 2023).

Finland has reduced the number of homeless people to 3,950 in 2021 with a goal of eradicating homelessness by 2027. The upfront costs of this solution were extensive; however, recent studies have shown that 15,000 euros "a year is saved for every homeless person in properly supported housing, considering the cost that would be otherwise incurred through emergency healthcare, social services, and criminal justice involvement" (Hancock, 2022). Finland is the only country in the European Union to see a dramatic decrease in homelessness, due to this solution and the work of the Y-Foundation, the nonprofit organization implementing the program across Finland. The Y-Foundation combines the Housing First program with other support services including employment, training, and access to other supporting resources (Hancock, 2022).

Housing First in Finland is a great example of a solution in the Prevent category. Finland saw a real need and for a few decades tried and failed to implement solutions. However, when they connected the true cause and symptoms of the problem, they were able to adopt a solution designed to directly impact the problem. The solution involves a large number of people, from employees of the Finnish government to nonprofit organizations like the Y-Foundation. The solution also took time to implement. It was a couple of years before Finland saw real progress from the program. The solution is also very expensive up front but does save money down the road (Hancock, 2022). If one of these elements was missing, the solution might not be as successful. It is the culmination of time, funding, and people that pave the way for this solution to be successful.

Before you commit to a solution in the Prevent category, make sure that you have ample access to time, people, and funding. You do not technically need all three depending on your problem but if you do not have access to any of these three items you will find more success in one of the other categories. However, if you have access to time, people, and funding you can design and implement an innovative successful solution in the Prevent category.

 FIRE DRILL!

Welcome to your next Fire Drill! You can now put into practice what you've learned by looking at your list of solutions and finding those that fit into the Prevent category. Scan the QR code to hear more detailed instructions from the author about the activities in this section.

kaylahholland.com/ puttingoutfires/audio

ADD SOLUTIONS TO THE PREVENT CATEGORY

The Prevent category includes solutions that completely solve the problem but require time, resources, and people. Look at the list of solutions you created in the Fire Drill! section of Chapter 4 and find those that fit into the Prevent category.

Prevent

EXPLORE SOLUTIONS

From the list of Prevent solutions above, select one specific solution. Answer the questions below to further explore your solution (Lewrick et al., 2020, p. 72, 108).

POF	What amounts of time, resources, and people will be needed for this solution?	
	Who does the solution impact?	
WHO	Who are the decision makers?	
	Who are the allies?	
	Who are the obstacles?	
	What happens once the solution is implemented?	
	What other symptoms are affected?	
WHAT	What are the positive interactions?	
	What are the negative interactions?	
	When will you know the solution is successful?	
WHEN	When will you know if adjustments need to be made to the solution?	
	How does the environment change when the solution is implemented?	
HOW	How does the solution directly impact the problem (cause, symptom, etc.)?	

LIKE, WISH, WONDER

Using the selected solution from the previous activity answer the three prompts in the activity below. What do you like about the solution (positive comments); what do you wish to see (positive criticisms); what do you wonder (questions) (Lewrick et al., 2020, p. 240).

LIKE

What do you like?
Positive comments

WISH

What do you wish?
Positive critiques

WONDER

What do you wonder?
Questions you have

SAMPLE PROBLEMS

Let's check in with our sample problems introduced in Chapter 2. How did the teacher and administrator complete the activities in the Fire Drill! section for this chapter?

TEACHER: PURPOSEFUL TECHNOLOGY USE TO ENHANCE STUDENT LEARNING

Looking at potential solutions that fit into the Prevent category helps to see which options might require large amounts of time, resources, and people. The teacher has listed seven solutions in the Prevent category and selects: "utilize AR and VR technologies to create immersive learning experiences, allowing students to explore complex concepts in a realistic environment."

Teacher's Prevent Solutions

Prevent

Develop educational apps that cater to various subjects, enabling students to learn at their own pace and in their own style.	Utilize AR and VR technologies to create immersive learning experiences, allowing students to explore complex concepts in a realistic environment.	Establish a support hotline or chat service where teachers can seek immediate assistance with technology-related issues.	Educate parents about the educational benefits of technology and involve them in their child's digital learning journey.
Advocate for universal internet access, ensuring that all students have equal opportunities to benefit from online resources.	Implement adaptive learning systems that assess students' abilities and tailor educational content to meet their specific needs and learning pace.	Collaborate with technology companies to provide schools with discounted or free access to educational software and hardware.	

The teacher explores the solution by answering several questions and listing what they like, wish, and wonder about the solution. For example, the teacher likes that this solution is not possible without technology but wonders if it is a purposeful use of technology or just using technology as a shiny new toy.

Teacher's Solution Exploration

POF	What amounts of time, resources, and people will be needed for this solution?	This solution requires funding to purchase devices and time to acquire devices and train people to use them.
WHO	Who does the solution impact?	The entire school
	Who are the decision makers?	Superintendent, principals, finance department
	Who are the allies?	Students and teachers
	Who are the obstacles?	Superintendent, finance department
WHAT	What happens once the solution is implemented?	Teachers can use AR and VR to enhance academic content.
	What other symptoms are affected?	Lack of engagement in content
	What are the positive interactions?	Students wanting to use AR/VR devices because they enjoy them
	What are the negative interactions?	Not tied to academics, seen as a standalone activity, requires a high level of tech skills to implement
WHEN	When will you know the solution is successful?	When teachers are using them often to bring academics to life in VR
	When will you know if adjustments need to be made to the solution?	When teachers return to their normal routine without using VR to enhance learning on a regular basis
HOW	How does the environment change when the solution is implemented?	It only changes for a short time while VR is being used
	How does the solution directly impact the problem (cause, symptom, etc.)?	The solution directly impacts the lack of student engagement by creating an interesting virtual environment for students.

Teacher's Like, Wish, Wonder Activity

LIKE

What do you like?
Positive comments

I like that this solution plunges into the digital world using VR.

WISH

What do you wish?
Positive critiques

I wish the solution created a larger and longer-lasting impact rather than just using VR. I can see some teachers using it once or twice and not on a regular basis.

WONDER

What do you wonder?
Questions you have

I wonder if this solution will actually affect the problem or just be a shiny new tech toy that is used a couple of times before teachers return to what is familiar.

 ## ISTE Standards: For Educators

2.2a: Shape, advance and accelerate a shared vision for empowered learning with technology by engaging with education stakeholders (ISTE, 2017).

2.6c: Create learning opportunities that challenge students to use a design process and computational thinking to innovate and solve problems (ISTE, 2017).

ADMINISTRATOR: ENSURING SCHOOLWIDE TECHNOLOGY PROGRAMS MEET THE NEEDS OF DIVERSE LEARNERS

Looking at potential solutions that fit into the Prevent category helps to select those that require large amounts of time, resources, and people. The administrator has listed seven solutions in the Prevent category and selects: "design classrooms and learning spaces that can be easily adapted to accommodate various learning styles and physical abilities."

Administrator's Prevent Solutions

Prevent

Integrate multilingual interfaces and support in educational software and devices to assist students who speak languages other than the primary language of instruction.	Implement UDL principles in technology programs, offering multiple means of representation, engagement, and expression to cater to diverse learning styles.	Design classrooms and learning spaces that can be easily adapted to accommodate various learning styles and physical abilities.	Implement learning management systems that are accessible to students with disabilities, ensuring they can fully participate in online learning activities.
Facilitate peer learning through collaborative online projects, allowing students to learn from each other and celebrate diversity.	Collaborate with educational technology companies to develop customized solutions that cater to the specific needs of diverse learners.	Implement peer evaluation methods where students provide feedback to each other, promoting empathy, understanding, and acceptance among diverse groups.	

The administrator explores further by answering several questions and listing what they like, wish, and wonder about the solution. For example, the administrator likes that this solution meets most needs of the learner whether physical, mental, or emotional, but wishes the solution could be implemented on a faster timeline.

Administrator's Solution Exploration

POF	What amounts of time, resources, and people will be needed for this solution?	This solution requires funding to purchase alternative furniture for classrooms, and other forms of technology and programs.
WHO	Who does the solution impact?	The entire school
	Who are the decision makers?	Superintendent, principals, finance department
	Who are the allies?	Students, teachers, principals, parents
	Who are the obstacles?	Finance department
WHAT	What happens once the solution is implemented?	Learning spaces become more welcoming to all types of student abilities (mental and physical) and all types of cultures and perspectives.
	What other symptoms are affected?	Student academics improve because superficial obstacles have been removed
	What are the positive interactions?	Students feel welcomed in the school and all classrooms.
	What are the negative interactions?	Takes a long time to implement because of funding and approval.
WHEN	When will you know the solution is successful?	When student academics improve and a welcoming environment is part of the school culture and core values
	When will you know if adjustments need to be made to the solution?	When students with diverse learning needs continue to struggle academically and/or students do not feel comfortable at school
HOW	How does the environment change when the solution is implemented?	The entire school culture changes dramatically because the needs of the students are now a main priority.
	How does the solution directly impact the problem (cause, symptom, etc.)?	The solution directly impacts the problem by removing superficial obstacles and ensuring all students are successful and feel welcome at school.

Administrator's Like, Wish, Wonder Activity

LIKE

What do you like?
Positive comments

I like that this solution really meets the true needs of all types of diverse learners whether the need is emotional, physical, or mental.

WISH

What do you wish?
Positive critiques

I wish the solution could be implemented on a faster timeline.

WONDER

What do you wonder?
Questions you have

I wonder if part of the solution could be implemented while waiting for approval, budgets, etc.

 ISTE Standards: For Education Leaders

3.2b: Engage education stakeholders in developing and adopting a shared vision for using technology to improve student success, informed by the learning sciences (ISTE, 2018).

3.5c: Use technology to regularly engage in reflective practices that support personal and professional growth (ISTE, 2018).

WHAT HAPPENS NEXT?

Now that you have explored solutions in all four categories of the *Putting Out Fires* Framework, it's time to put your firefighting skills to the test by conquering the flames and implementing your own solution. Select a solution from any of the four categories and continue to the next chapter to finally put out the fire!

CHAPTER 9
PUTTING OUT THE FIRE

YOU HAVE COMPLETED NUMEROUS ACTIVITIES in this book including selecting a problem that affects the most people, looking at all people affected by the problem, creating "one hundred" solutions, and categorizing those solutions to select the best possible solution for your problem. If implementing the solution were solely up to you, I feel confident you would find a way to be successful. However, most likely the solution involves other people. Change will likely be required, and we all know that people typically resist change. How, then, can we set the solution up for success if it relies on fallible people changing?

CLEAR THE PATH

In the book *Switch*, Chip and Dan Heath (2011) discuss how to create change when change is hard by exploring the idea of the elephant, the rider, and the path. The Heath brothers obtained this visual from another book titled *The Happiness Hypothesis* by Jonathan Haidt. The elephant represents our emotional side, and the rider represents our rational side (Heath & Heath, 2011). The rider holds the reins, but the elephant essentially determines the direction. If the elephant and rider disagree, the rider loses to the extremely large elephant (Heath & Heath, 2011). All of us have experienced situations where the rider and the elephant have disagreed on a direction. The elephant overpowering the rider represents our emotions overpowering our logic. The elephant is in control if you have ever "slept-in, overeaten, tried to quit smoking and failed, skipped the gym, gotten angry, [or] said something you regretted" (Heath & Heath, p. 7, 2011). When the elephant is in control, we look "for a quick payoff (ice cream cone) over the long-term payoff (being thin)" (Heath & Heath, p. 7, 2011). In contrast, the rider overpowering the elephant represents logic overpowering emotions. Some riders tend to constantly "over-analyze and overthink" (Heath & Heath, p. 8, 2011). The overthinker might agonize for "twenty minutes about what to eat for dinner…[and] brainstorm new ideas for hours" without taking a first step (Heath & Heath, p. 8, 2011).

When implementing solutions that will inevitably require big changes, we must address both types of people: the elephants and the riders. The "Rider provides the planning and direction, and the Elephant provides the energy" (Heath & Heath, p. 8, 2011). According to the Heath brothers, "If you reach the Riders of your team but not the Elephants, team members will have understanding without motivation. If you reach the Elephants but not their Riders, they'll have passion without direction" (p. 8). When directing the rider (logic), we need to "provide crystal clear direction" (Heath & Heath, p. 17, 2011). When motivating the elephant (emotions), we need to "engage people's emotional side" through stories, visuals, and data (Heath & Heath, p. 17, 2011).

Another crucial piece of this metaphor is the path. We cannot expect the elephant and the rider to move forward together if the path is not clear. The path is the overall situation. "What looks like a people problem is often a situation problem" (Heath & Heath, p. 18, 2011). To clear the path, we need to remove obstacles from the situation so the elephant and rider can more freely move forward together.

In Lordstown, Ohio, "Pattie Poppe is a department manager at the General Motors automotive plant" (Heath & Heath, p. 213, 2011). Her problem is how to best roll out a new policy for wearing safety equipment. This change is extremely important given that the old policy allowed employees to opt out of wearing the appropriate safety equipment, because the old policy was complicated, and workers felt the policy did not apply directly to them (Heath & Heath, 2011). To direct the rider (appeal to logic), Poppe removed the old complex policy and created a new policy with two rules "(1) Everyone is required to wear hard side shields and safety glasses (2) No one can expose any bare skin (no shorts or short-sleeve shirts)" (Heath & Heath, p. 214, 2011). This rule applied to all employees in the plant and mitigated the issue from the older policy, that employees felt the rules did not apply to them (Heath & Heath, 2011). To motivate the elephant (appeal to emotion), Poppe found safety glasses with a more acceptable, up-to-date design (Heath & Heath, 2011). To shape the path (clear obstacles), Poppe painted a large blue line around the exterior of the plant and posted life-size posters of blue men correctly wearing all safety gear at every entrance, triggering employees to suit up in their protective gear upon arrival (Heath & Heath, 2011). Poppe wrote two simple directions, purchased new equipment that was more acceptable to employees, and clearly defined expectations by requiring all employees to don protective gear when crossing the blue line. This solution is a great example of addressing logic, emotion, and obstacles as part of planning and implementation.

You may be asking yourself, what in the world do elephants, riders, and paths have to do with implementing a solution? Clearing the path and understanding the emotions and logic of the people involved in a problem are crucial steps for successful implementation of your solution. In order to create change, we must address both the logical side of people as well as the emotional side. People are usually afraid of change. The fear they feel is their elephant. No matter how detailed the logic is behind the change, their fear must be addressed. We must also provide clear direction for implementing the solution. Logical people will feel lost when confronting confusing or conflicting information. Once we address feelings and provide clear direction, we must clear the path of obstacles. Completing all three of these steps allows us to implement the solution in the best way possible while keeping people at the center of the implementation strategy.

IMPLEMENTATION STRATEGIES

Before you begin addressing the emotions and logic of the people involved and clearing the path, you need to map out what the solution implementation will look like. You cannot address the emotions and logic of people you do not realize are involved. You also cannot clear the path without first mapping out the route. Therefore, your first step will be to picture the end result of your implemented solution and work backwards to determine how you will best reach the end.

To better understand this concept, think about the steps required to result in your morning cup of coffee. In the blank space provided, map out the steps needed in order to get your cup of coffee.

There is no right or wrong way to start. This exercise helps us determine how far back we go when thinking about steps in a process. This type of exercise is called distribution prototyping—it can be completed with any process. Distribution prototyping is popular as a design-thinking exercise and is most often used when mapping out the process for creating toast (Greenberg et al., 2021, p. 184). As a fan of coffee, I thought this was an excellent modification of the usual design-thinking exercise.

Some of you may have started your morning cup of coffee at the point where you pour coffee into your cup. Others may have started with turning on the coffee pot. Still others might have started at the grocery store, purchasing the ground coffee beans, and others still might have begun all the way back when the coffee bean was first plucked from the tree. Now, turn the page to see an example (**Figure 9.1**).

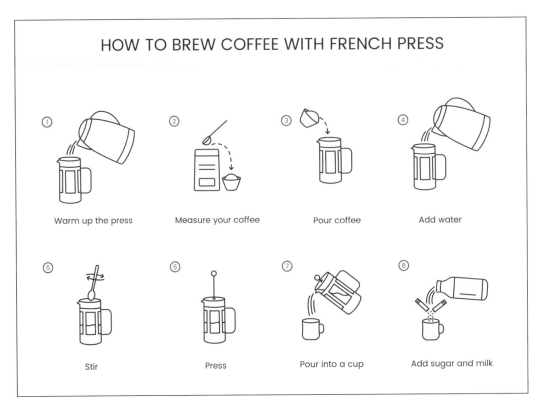

HOW TO BREW COFFEE WITH FRENCH PRESS

① Warm up the press

② Measure your coffee

③ Pour coffee

④ Add water

⑤ Stir

⑥ Press

⑦ Pour into a cup

⑧ Add sugar and milk

FIGURE 9.1 One example of the steps leading to a morning cup of coffee.

When considering the implementation of your solution, you should consider all the steps necessary to best clear the path for the elephants and riders involved. How many steps are necessary to implement your solution? For some, your solution is simple, much like the automotive plant removing complicated and confusing policies and instead creating a clearly defined culture of expectations. For others, your solution requires more steps in the implementation process. Much like the coffee exercise, there is no right or wrong way to begin. We simply need to ensure all steps are being addressed to give our solution the best possible chance of success.

🔔 FIRE DRILL!

Welcome to your next Fire Drill! You can now put into practice what you've learned throughout this chapter, including addressing your elephants and riders and creating steps to clear the path. Scan the QR code to hear more detailed instructions from the author about the activities in this section.

**kaylahholland.com/
puttingoutfires/audio**

CLEAR THE PATH

To get started implementing your solution, you must first consider the entire path using distribution prototyping (Greenberg et al., 2021, p. 184). When completing this exercise, you should also consider the feelings and logic involved with the implementation. Fill in the spaces below to consider the entire path required to implement this solution.

ELEPHANT	What emotions will be involved in the implementation of the solution?	
	Who are the people driven by emotions?	
	How can you best address the emotions involved?	
RIDER	What logic will be involved in the implementation of the solution?	
	Who are the people driven by logic?	
	How can you best address the logic involved?	
PATH	Using distribution prototyping (see Figure 9.1), create a step-by-step process outlining the path for implementation. What obstacles are present? How will you address the obstacles and clear the path?	

5X5X5 METHOD

Often, there are so many ways to get started we struggle to take the first step. In the blanks below, write down the steps you will need to complete in the next 5 days, then 5 weeks, then 5 months, to successfully implement your selected solution. Breaking down your entire implementation into these three steps encourages us to take the first step.

> **5 Days:**

> **5 Weeks:**

> **5 Months:**

SAMPLE PROBLEMS

Let's check in with our sample problems introduced in Chapter 2. How did the teacher and administrator complete the activities in the Fire Drill! section for this chapter?

TEACHER: PURPOSEFUL TECHNOLOGY USE TO ENHANCE STUDENT LEARNING

The solution the teacher selected is from the Contain category and includes fostering purposeful use of technology by participating in workshops on the effective use of technology in the classroom, joining other experienced teachers in a personal learning network to learn best practices, and finally designing lessons that implement the purposeful use of technology in the classroom to enhance student learning. Completing the clearing the path activity highlights the areas of emotions and logic needing to be addressed by the selected solution, and helps the teacher plan to successfully clear the path of any obstacles.

The teacher then creates three practical steps to move forward with implementing the solution over the next five months. This solution is the best possible path forward to answering the *how might we* statement created in Chapter 3:

> **TEACHER:** How might we improve classroom instruction for students to engage them in lessons that are relevant and meaningful?

Teacher's Clear the Path Activity

ELEPHANT	What emotions will be involved in the implementation of the solution?	Fear of the unknown and change, uncomfortable feelings when trying something new, fear of failure and making mistakes
	Who are the people driven by emotions?	Teachers
	How can you best address the emotions involved?	Attend workshops to learn best practices, and obtain a mentor to help lessen the fear
RIDER	What logic will be involved in the implementation of the solution?	Including content and technology, and changing the teaching style to what is best for the students
	Who are the people driven by logic?	Teachers, students, principals
	How can you best address the logic involved?	Creating a "one new thing" mentality to avoid getting overwhelmed.
PATH	Using distribution prototyping (see Figure 9.1), create a step-by-step process outlining the path for implementation. What obstacles are present? How will you address the obstacles and clear the path?	

	1. Attend a workshop on edtech best practices.	2. Join a PLN to chat with an experienced teacher/mentor.	3. Select one new digital tool or a new way of designing lessons using technology.	4. Practice the tool/lesson with one class.	5. Make needed changes and implement in all classes.

The obstacles are finding the right workshops and mentor/teacher/PLN, and finding time to do both of those things. Obstacles can be addressed by making a list of available workshops and PLNs and slowly working through them until the best fit is found. Once a new tool/lesson is selected, the obstacle will be choosing when and how to use it in class. Trying it out with one period first will address the obstacle of feeling overwhelmed.

Teacher's 5x5x5 Method

5 Days: Create a list of available workshops and PLNs.

5 Weeks: Attend at least four workshops and meet at least once with a mentor.

5 Months: Select a digital tool or new lesson design and implement it in the classroom at least three times; first with one period and then with all classes. Obtain feedback, make changes, and implement again.

ISTE Standards: For Educators

2.2b: Advocate for equitable access to educational technology, digital content and learning opportunities to meet the diverse needs of all students (ISTE, 2017).

2.4c: Use collaborative tools to expand students' authentic, real-world learning experiences by engaging virtually with experts, teams and students, locally and globally (ISTE, 2017).

2.6b: Manage the use of technology and student learning strategies in digital platforms, virtual environments, hands-on makerspaces or in the field (ISTE, 2017).

ADMINISTRATOR: ENSURING SCHOOLWIDE TECHNOLOGY PROGRAMS MEET THE NEEDS OF DIVERSE LEARNERS

The administrator opted to merge several solutions from the Detect category together to create one path forward to solving the problem. The administrator recognized the immediate need of providing training for teachers to understand and respect diverse cultural backgrounds, and provided workshops to enhance the skills of teachers in using adaptive technologies to accommodate diverse learners. After collecting data on how technology can be used to meet the needs of all learners, the administrator put policies in place to ensure technology use is respectful of all cultures, creating a welcoming environment for all students. Completing the Clearing the Path activity highlighted the areas of emotions and logic needing to be addressed by the selected solution, and explored how to successfully clear the path of any obstacles. The administrator then created three practical steps to move forward with implementing the solution over the next five months. This solution is the best possible path forward to answering the *how might we* statement created in Chapter 3:

> **ADMINISTRATOR:** How might we improve digital programming for all students to meet the diverse needs that currently exist?

Administrator's Clear the Path Activity

ELEPHANT	What emotions will be involved in the implementation of the solution?	Fear of making mistakes, exhaustion from too many things at once, fear of feeling uncomfortable when addressing biases.
	Who are the people driven by emotions?	Teachers, students
	How can you best address the emotions involved?	Attend workshops to learn best practices, and obtain a mentor to help lessen the fear
RIDER	What logic will be involved in the implementation of the solution?	Creating a safe and welcoming space for everyone is crucial to the academic success of students
	Who are the people driven by logic?	Teachers, students, principals
	How can you best address the logic involved?	Starting slow, big changes take time; ensuring all voices are heard

PATH

Using distribution prototyping, create a step-by-step process outlining the path for implementation. What obstacles are present? How will you address them and clear the path?

1. Find an expert to provide a workshop.	2. Host a workshop on respecting cultures and adaptive tech.	3. Collect data on how tech is currently being used. Acknowledge existing gaps.	4. Create a place for all voices to be heard when exploring the data.	5. Together, create a solution to fill gaps and institute a culture of belonging.

The obstacles are finding the expert to provide the workshop and getting everyone on board with such a large change. Addressing the obstacles can be done by reaching out to my network of people, and creating a small committee of teachers and students to help drive the change appropriately.

Administrator's 5x5x5 Method

5 Days: Create a list of appropriate experts to provide the webinar.

5 Weeks: Create a small committee of both teachers and students to select the expert and host the workshop.

5 Months: Collect data on how technology is currently being used; using the data, have the committee create a two-year plan to implement changes so that our school becomes a welcoming environment that uses technology correctly to remove learning obstacles from students.

 ISTE Standards: For Education Leaders

3.1a: Ensure all students have skilled teachers who actively use technology to meet student learning needs (ISTE, 2018).

3.2b: Build on the shared vision by collaboratively creating a strategic plan that articulates how technology will be used to enhance learning (ISTE, 2018).

3.3a: Empower educators to exercise professional agency, build teacher leadership skills and pursue personalized professional learning (ISTE, 2018).

WHAT HAPPENS NEXT?

Now, put this plan into action and implement the solution you have designed. When implementing your solution, make sure you are addressing all the elephants and the riders while clearing the path.

The smoke is beginning to clear; let's determine if the solution was successful.

CHAPTER 10
WHEN THE SMOKE CLEARS

ONCE YOU HAVE IMPLEMENTED YOUR SOLUTION, and the metaphorical smoke clears from the raging fire that was your problem, you can complete the next step. Notice that I did not say the final step. This process will always be evolving as you continue to check in on the solution you implemented, but more on that later. The next step is to obtain feedback from the people impacted by the problem and the solution. Obtaining feedback directly from the people you designed the solution for allows you to ensure your solution is successfully impacting the problem and is not in fact bringing harm to those involved.

OBTAINING FEEDBACK

Feedback can be obtained in many forms, including focus groups, surveys, visual observations, feedback loops, and more. Regardless of the feedback option you choose, the overall goal is for every voice impacted by the problem and solution to be heard and valued. If the feedback is not positive, adjust the solution where needed and implement it again.

An example of implementing a solution not designed for the clients involved can be found at the airport in Houston, Texas. Executives at this airport were perplexed about the large number of complaints lodged by passengers about the long wait times in the baggage claim area. To address these complaints, the executives immediately increased the number of personnel working shifts as baggage handlers; however, the complaints continued. The executives then completed a thorough on-site analysis of the baggage complaint problem and "discovered that it took passengers only one minute to walk from their gate to baggage claim, but seven more minutes to collect their bags" (Gabr-Ryn, 2018). Essentially, passengers were quickly arriving in the baggage claim area but needed to wait almost seven minutes before their bags arrived. After this discovery, the executives decided to move the "arrival gate further away from the main terminal, and then routed the bags to the outermost carousel. Passengers now spent a total of six minutes walking, and spent just two minutes waiting for their bags" (Gabr-Ryn, 2018). The number of complaints "immediately dropped to zero" (Gabr-Ryn, 2018). While this solution is effective at lowering the number of complaints received, it does not actually solve the problem. It simply reroutes the problem and manipulates the clients (passengers) to think their wait time is less when in reality the wait time is the same as it was before.

If the executives had obtained feedback on this solution, the passengers would have been able to voice their concerns over now being asked to walk six times farther (one minute to six minutes) than before. The issue was not the walking time but the waiting time.

The executives did not keep their clients in mind when designing this solution. However, they feel they solved the problem successfully simply because the number of complaints dropped to zero.

We must obtain feedback from all people impacted by the problem and the solution so that we can determine if the implemented solution does in fact solve the problem. We do not want to be the executives from the Houston, Texas, airport manipulating our clients to believe we solved the problem when in fact we are bringing harm to them by forcing them to walk six times farther.

REFLECTING ON THE PROCESS

Once you are satisfied the solution in place is in fact successful and no longer needs to be tweaked, you can reflect on the overall process. In Chapter 3, we discussed how this process is a journey—long and arduous, or enjoyable and rewarding, but a journey nonetheless. I hope that you are excited about the solution you implemented and relieved to have brought positive change to the people impacted.

If someone asks you about the solution, how will you respond? Can your creative brain summarize the journey into a few helpful sentences? Often, those outside the creative process of implementing the solution struggle to see the beauty in its success (Greenberg et al., 2021). We need to draw them a map. Creating a map highlighting both the highs and lows honors your journey and paints the picture of the process so that others can celebrate with you. Your final activity in the Fire Drill! section of this chapter will be to map this journey in order to see how far you've come in implementing the solution and to provide clear steps that you can share with others.

As I stated at the beginning of this chapter, this process will always be evolving. If you fail to check in with your problem and solution from time to time, you run the risk of the problem happening again. I do not mean checking in within the next couple of weeks; I mean not checking in for several months. However, most of the problems we face were once solved by someone years, perhaps decades, ago. The problems have returned because the solutions implemented years ago are no longer viable for the clients currently experiencing them. I hope this fact intrigues—rather than overwhelms—you. Problems will always exist. With the new mindset and toolkit provided by this book, you can tackle any problem with excitement, no matter how large or small.

🔔 FIRE DRILL!

Welcome to your final Fire Drill! You can now put into practice what you've learned throughout this chapter including obtaining feedback on your solution and creating your journey map. Scan the QR code to hear more detailed instructions from the author about the activities in this section.

kaylahholland.com/ puttingoutfires/audio

FEEDBACK GRID

It is extremely important that you obtain feedback from all clients involved in the problem and the solution. The way you obtain feedback is not important, so you can obtain feedback in any way you would like. Complete the grid below while reflecting on the solution you implemented. There are four items to consider (Lewrick et al., 2020, p. 218).

1. The heart represents love—what are the things you love about this solution? What works well?

2. The flag represents critiques—what are the things you *didn't* love? What isn't working?

3. The speech bubbles represent questions—what questions do you have about the solution?

4. The target represents ideas—what are ways you can make improvements to the solution?

WHAT WENT DOWN

For your final activity, create a journey map honoring the highs and lows you have experienced by solving this problem. Using the space and the horizontal line on the next page, begin at the farthest point on the left and create a timeline for your process. The horizontal line represents a middle level for your feelings. Begin to map your journey by adding in key moments and placing them above or below the horizontal line, depending on how high or low you felt when that moment occurred. Once you have mapped all key moments from the process, draw a box around both your highest high and your lowest low. These two moments should be shared every time you relate your story to someone (Greenberg et al., 2021, p. 215).

IDEAS YOU LOVE ♡	⬗ POSITIVE CRITICISMS
QUESTIONS YOU HAVE 💬	◎ IDEAS TO MAKE IT BETTER

SAMPLE PROBLEMS

Let's check in with our sample problems introduced in Chapter 2. How did the teacher and administrator complete the activities in the Fire Drill! section for this chapter?

TEACHER: PURPOSEFUL TECHNOLOGY USE TO ENHANCE STUDENT LEARNING

The teacher loved that the chosen solution did not feel overwhelming, but when implementing again would opt to add more than one new thing within the five-month timeline. When reflecting on how the solution was implemented, the teacher's low was having to make changes after implementing the digital tool for the first time. The high for the teacher was feeling confident enough to implement the new lesson in all classes. The teacher's problem is a great example of how a Contain solution is helpful because starting small and trying one new thing at a time can be extremely impactful. The teacher essentially contained the problem for now, and if the teacher continues implementing new types of lessons utilizing technology their teaching style will be completely different in one or two years. The Contain solution helps the teacher create impactful change without feeling overwhelmed. The change will be authentic and will put the needs of students first.

Teacher's Feedback Grid

I love that this solution didn't feel overwhelming.	The process was extremely slow and only implemented in one lesson.
IDEAS YOU LOVE ♡	🔖 POSITIVE CRITICISMS
QUESTIONS YOU HAVE	 IDEAS TO MAKE IT BETTER
How can this solution be replicated to truly change the culture of the classroom and use technology with purpose to enhance student learning?	I will implement this solution again but instead of one new thing, I will complete the five-month timeline implementing at least five new digital tools and/or new lesson designs.

Teacher's Journey Map

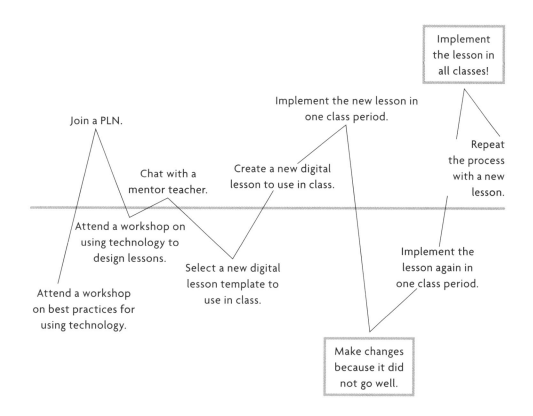

Join a PLN.

Implement the new lesson in
one class period.

Implement
the lesson in
all classes!

Chat with a
mentor teacher.

Create a new digital
lesson to use in class.

Repeat
the process
with a new
lesson.

Attend a workshop on
using technology to
design lessons.

Select a new digital
lesson template to
use in class.

Implement the
lesson again in
one class period.

Attend a workshop
on best practices for
using technology.

Make changes
because it did
not go well.

 ISTE Standards: For Educators

2.1a: Set professional learning goals to explore and apply pedagogical approaches made possible by technology and reflect on their effectiveness (ISTE, 2017).

2.1b: Pursue professional interests by creating and actively participating in local and global learning networks (ISTE, 2017).

2.6a: Foster a culture where students take ownership of their learning goals and outcomes in both independent and group settings (ISTE, 2017).

ADMINISTRATOR: ENSURING SCHOOLWIDE TECHNOLOGY PROGRAMS MEET THE NEEDS OF DIVERSE LEARNERS

The administrator loved that the chosen solution felt authentic and included all voices, but realized the staff needed an entire semester-long workshop to truly implement the solution. When looking back over how the solution was implemented, the administrator's low was when the collected data showed how much improvement was really needed. The high for the administrator was when the committee became invested in the solution and completed a practical two-year plan that showed how impactful change was possible. The administrator's problem is a great example of how using a Detect solution can be extremely helpful, because instead of attempting to solve the problem immediately, the administrator studied the problem, brought others on board, and created a solution that allowed for significant change to happen over a two-year period. While this solution could not be quickly implemented, it does solve the problem by addressing the cause and creating a space where all types of learners can succeed.

Administrator's Feedback Grid

I love that this solution included all voices and felt authentic. IDEAS YOU LOVE ♡	More than one workshop was needed to get teachers on board. ⛉ POSITIVE CRITICISMS
QUESTIONS YOU HAVE 💬 How can we keep the momentum going throughout the two-year plan?	◎ IDEAS TO MAKE IT BETTER Providing more than one workshop, perhaps a semester of staff development, to better understand the nuances to this problem.

Administrator's Journey Map

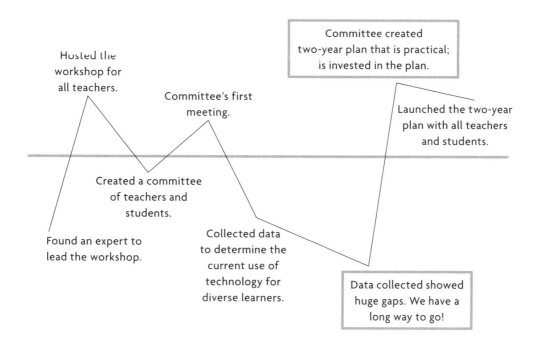

 ISTE Standards: For Education Leaders

3.2c: Evaluate progress on the strategic plan, make course corrections, measure impact and scale effective approaches for using technology to transform learning (ISTE, 2018).

3.2d: Communicate effectively with stakeholders to gather input on the plan, celebrate successes and engage in a continuous improvement cycle (ISTE, 2018).

3.4a: Lead teams to collaboratively establish robust infrastructure and systems needed to implement the strategic plan. (ISTE, 2018).

CONCLUSION

WHAT HAPPENS NEXT?

Congratulations! You did it! You completed the entire *Putting Out Fires* process and solved a real problem you were facing with a practical solution that keeps people at the center. This same process can be used over and over for all problems you face, both big and small, professional and personal. Do you need to complete this entire process every time you want to solve a problem? No, but I hope that completing this process has reframed the way you view problems, potential solutions, and the people impacted by both. For all future problems, you can quickly walk through most of these exercises using a streamlined digital version. You can access the streamlined framework on the website at **www.kaylahholland.com/puttingoutfires**.

Thank you for sticking with me on this journey. I truly hope that you have been able to implement a real solution to a challenging problem. I also hope that you continue to view challenges as opportunities to be creative: implementing innovative solutions that keep people at the center and create a better world for us all.

Here's to many more innovative solutions implemented for challenging problems in the future. May you emerge victorious as you conquer the problems that lie ahead.

Happy solving,

Kaylah

REFERENCES

Adams, C. (2023, August 1). *Some Houston School Libraries will become disciplinary spaces.* NBCNews.com. https://www.nbcnews.com/news/nbcblk/houston-school-libraries-will-become-disciplinary-spaces-rcna97394

Ben-Ur, E. (2020). Innovators' Compass. https://innovatorscompass.org/

Bogost, I. (2023, May 23). The first year of AI college ends in ruin. *The Atlantic.*

Bolger, M. (2022, April 13). Facilitator cards. https://www.facilitator.cards/cards/

Dam, R. F., & Siang, T. Y. (2022, September 10). *The history of design thinking.* The Interaction Design Foundation. https://www.interaction-design.org/literature/article/design-thinking-get-a-quick-overview-of-the-history

Duran, C. (2023, July 29). Stanford startup aims to make assistive technology affordable. *The Stanford Daily.*

Evans, J. (2022, September 15). New glow-in-the-dark Australian road feature goes viral. *News.Com.Au.*

Gabr-Ryn, B. (2018, August 25). The issue at Houston Airport: Occupied time and design. *Medium.*

Goodman, J. D. (2023, August 13). Texas revamps Houston schools, closing libraries and angering parents. *The New York Times.*

Gladwell, M. (2002). *The Tipping Point.* Little, Brown and Company.

Glösel, K. (2023, June 26). Finland ends homelessness and provides shelter for all in need. *The Mandarin.*

Greenberg, S. S., Kelley, D., & Hirshon, M. (2021). *Creative acts for curious people: How to think, create, and lead in unconventional ways.* Ten Speed Press.

Hancock, E. (2022, October 6). Helsinki is still leading the way in ending homelessness—but how are they doing it? *World Habitat.*

Heath, C., & Heath, D. (2011). *Switch: How to change things when change is hard.* Broadway Books.

Heath, D. (2020). *Upstream: The quest to solve problems before they happen.* Avid Reader Press.

International Fire Safety Standards Coalition. (2020, October). International fire safety standards: Common principles. https://unece.org/fileadmin/DAM/hlm/documents/Standards/UNECE_International_Fire_Safety_Standards_October_2020.pdf

International Society for Technology in Education. (2017). ISTE Standards for Educators. https://www.iste.org/standards/iste-standards-for-teachers

International Society for Technology in Education. (2018). ISTE Standards for Education Leaders. https://iste.org/standards/iste-standards-for-education-leaders

IDEO. (n.d.). IDEO design thinking. IDEO. https://designthinking.ideo.com/

Lewrick, M., Link, P., & Leifer, L. (2020). *The design thinking toolbox: A guide to mastering the most popular and valuable innovation methods*. Wiley.

Modal: NFCC CPO (n.d.). Control Measure Knowledge. (n.d.). https://www.ukfrs.com/modal/general-cm/13785/313689/document/nojs

Munetsi, E., Simms, et al. (2018, February 8). Trained lay health workers reduce common mental disorder symptoms of adults with suicidal ideation in Zimbabwe: A cohort study. *BioMed Central*.

Nereim, V. (2023, August 28). To escape the heat in Dubai, head to the beach at midnight. *The New York Times*.

Palmer, E. (1973). Formative research in the production of television for children. Children's Television Workshop.

Reid, A. A. (2023, December 21). *DeJuan Strickland honored for his ingenuity. St. Louis American*.

Samuel, K. (2023, February 3). A group of grandmothers in Zimbabwe is helping the world reimagine mental health care. *The Boston Globe*.

Schaffner, A. K. (2023, July 6). Understanding the circles of influence, concern, and control. PositivePsychology.com.

Schapova, N. (2022, September 21). Glow-in-the-dark roads trialled to reduce road toll, protect wildlife. ABC News.

Tsui, E. (2023, July 26). Harnessing green energy from everyday commutes: A case study of Paris's innovative mini turbines. *Medium*.

Weiner, S. (2022, August 9). A growing psychiatrist shortage and an enormous demand for mental health services. AAMC.

Wise, S. (2022). *Design for belonging: How to build inclusion and collaboration in your communities*. Ten Speed Press.

Verhey R. et al. Potential resilience to post-traumatic stress disorder and common mental disorders among lay health workers working on the Friendship Bench Programme in Zimbabwe. Journal of Health Care for the Poor and Underserved.

Voelkert, J. C. (2015). Fire and fire extinguishment. https://amerex-fire.com/upl/downloads/educational-documents/fire-and-fire-extinguishment-99cd88b2.pdf

INDEX

#

5x5x5 method, 123, 126, 128

B

Ben-Ur, Ela, 34–35
Blue's Clues, 78
Brown, Tim, 3

C

capacity and influence, 21, 48–49, 52–53,
    55–56, 58–59
Chibanda, Dixon, 64–65
clearing the path, 118–28
clients, 36–37, 130–32
Contain (solution category), 46–47, 90–101
cooling method, 62
    See also Extinguish (solution category)
Crawford, Kat, v, x

D

Design for Belonging, 34
design thinking, 3–4, 34, 121
Detect (solution category), 46–47, 76–87

E

elephant and rider, 118–28
empathy map, 38–42
    See also clients
Extinguish (solution category), 46–47, 62–74

F

feedback, 130–37
five whys, 25, 28, 31
Friendship Bench, 64–65

G

Gladwell, Malcolm, 78
Google Docs, 19

H

Haidt, Jonathan, 118
Happiness Hypothesis, The, 118
Heath, Chip, 118–20
Heath, Dan, 14–19, 35, 118–20
Housing First, 106–7
Houston, Texas, 35, 130–31
how might we statements, 38–43
Hudson, Jennifer, 16

I

IDEO, 3–4
impact of problems, 20–30
influence and problems, 21–30, 48–49, 52–53,
    55–56, 58–59
Innovators' Compass, 34–35
interrupting method, 104
    See also Prevent (solution category)
IQuadrant activity, 23–30
ISTE Standards for Education Leaders, 7, 31,
    43, 59, 74, 87, 101, 116, 128, 137
ISTE Standards for Educators, 7, 28, 41, 56, 71,
    84, 98, 113, 126, 135

J

journey maps, 133, 135, 137

L

Lawson, Bryan, 3
like, wish, and wonder activity
    Contain and, 95, 101
    Detect and, 81, 83, 87
    Extinguish and, 68, 71, 74
    Prevent and, 110, 113, 116

M

Miles, Mike, 35–36
Munetsi, Epiphany, 64

O

one hundred ideas activity, 50–51, 54, 57

P

Palmer, Edward, 77–78
path, clearing the, 118–28
people lists, 37, 39–42
Prevent (solution category), 46–47, 104–16
problem blindness, 17–18, 24, 27, 30
problem ownership, lack of, 18–19, 24, 27, 30
problem-solving process, 4–5
prototyping, 121, 123
Putting Out Fires framework, 4–5, 46–48

R

reflection, 131–37
rider and elephant, 118–28
root causes, 25, 28, 31
    See also upstream thinking

S

sample problem for administrators, 11, 29–31,
    41–43, 71–73, 84–87, 98–101, 113–16,
    126–28, 136–37
sample problem for teachers, 11, 26–28, 39–41,
    53–56, 68–71, 81–84, 95–98, 110–13,
    124–26, 134–35
Sciences of the Artificial, The, 3
secure schools, x, 2, 17–18, 63, 77, 91, 100
Sesame Street, 78
Simon, Herbert A., 3
smothering method, 76
    See also Detect (solution category)

stakeholders. *See* clients
starvation method, 90
    See also Contain (solution category)
⬛⬛⬛⬛⬛, ⬛⬛⬛⬛⬛, ⬛⬛ ⬛⬛
Switch, 118

T

Tarmac Linemarking, 91–92
Tech Boy Lunch Heroes, 16–17
thinking and feeling activity, 7–8
Time, 16
Tipping Point, The, 78
TranscribeGlass, 16
Tsui, Eddie, 15

U

Upstream, 14–19, 35
upstream thinking, 14–19
    See also root causes

V

Verhey, Ruth, 64
VR (virtual reality), 105

W

Weiner, Stacy, 64–65
Wise, Susie, 34

Y

Y-Foundation, 106

Z

Zola, Irving, 14–15